4 —

Praise for *Spiritual Politics*

"*Spiritual Politics* is an informed and insightful telling of the story of American religion and public life over the last four decades. Mark Silk brilliantly depicts the shifts and churnings of moral passion and pretension in the life of an incorrigibly religious people. This book should establish itself as a lively reference in discussions about a nation ever in search of what it uncertainly believes to be its destiny."

—Richard John Neuhaus
The Center on Religion & Society

"Mark Silk's witty and engrossing book demonstrates at once the pervasiveness of evangelical religion and politics in American life and the paradoxes that have resulted since 1945 from the nation's alleged commitment to the 'Judeo-Christian' tradition. *Spiritual Politics* draws attention to people and movements that haven't received the public attention they deserve."

—Daniel Aaron
*Department of English and American
Literature and Language
Harvard University*

■

Other Books by Mark Silk

(with Leonard Silk) THE AMERICAN ESTABLISHMENT

SPIRITUAL

POLITICS

∎

RELIGION
AND
AMERICA
SINCE
WORLD WAR II

∎

MARK
SILK

A TOUCHSTONE BOOK
PUBLISHED BY
SIMON & SCHUSTER INC.
NEW YORK LONDON TORONTO SYDNEY TOKYO

TOUCHSTONE
SIMON & SCHUSTER BUILDING
ROCKEFELLER CENTER
1230 AVENUE OF THE AMERICAS
NEW YORK, NEW YORK 10020
COPYRIGHT © 1988 BY MARK SILK
ALL RIGHTS RESERVED
INCLUDING THE RIGHT OF REPRODUCTION
IN WHOLE OR IN PART IN ANY FORM
FIRST TOUCHSTONE EDITION 1989
TOUCHSTONE AND COLOPHON
ARE REGISTERED TRADEMARKS
OF SIMON & SCHUSTER INC.
DESIGNED BY KAROLINA HARRIS
MANUFACTURED IN THE UNITED STATES OF AMERICA

10 9 8 7 6 5 4 3 2 1

LIBRARY OF CONGRESS CATALOGING
IN PUBLICATION DATA
SILK, MARK.

SPIRITUAL POLITICS: RELIGION AND AMERICA SINCE WORLD WAR II /
MARK SILK.—1ST TOUCHSTONE ED.
    P.   CM.—(A TOUCHSTONE BOOK)
    BIBLIOGRAPHY: P.
    INCLUDES INDEX.
    1. RELIGION AND POLITICS—UNITED STATES—HISTORY—20TH
CENTURY. 2. UNITED STATES—RELIGION—1945–   I. TITLE.
BL2525.S55 1989   88-39601
261.7'0973—DC19   CIP
ISBN 0-671-43910-3
    0-671-67563-X PBK.

▪ ACKNOWLEDGMENT

T H I S short book has been long in the making. My first thanks go to Giles Constable and Caroline Walker Bynum: *de verbis et exemplis me docuerunt.* William Hutchison ushered a sometime medievalist into the mysteries of American religious history; he and the other members of the New World Colloquium at the Harvard Divinity School, before whom I put a good deal of what follows, provided instruction and collegiality of a special kind. Helpful advice and counsel came from Leonard Bushkoff, Jacob Cohen, Dieter Georgi, Mitchell Miller, Jon Roberts, Werner Sollors, and the two anonymous referees of my 1984 *American Quarterly* article "Notes on the Judeo-Christian Tradition in America," the bulk of which has, in one form or another, found its way into these pages. The 1985 Harvard-Lilly Endowment project on mainline Protestantism provided the opportunity, and support, for archival research into the relations between Billy Graham and the National Council of Churches. Robert Gorham Davis, Alfred Kazin, and Adam Silk read drafts and offered welcome encouragement. Robert Asahina has been an editor of remarkable patience and care. Above all, I want to thank my wife, Tema Kaiser Silk, whose love and good sense sustain me in all things.

■

For Leonard and Abraham

grandfather and grandson

■ CONTENTS

INTRODUCTION: SPIRITUAL POLITICS   15

1 THE AGE OF ANXIETY   23

2 A NEW CREED   40

3 THE WAGES OF CONVERSION (I)   54

4 THE WAGES OF CONVERSION (II)   70

5 WARS OF FAITH   87

6 WHO SHALL OVERCOME   108

7 BREAKING THROUGH   136

8 A PLURAL MAJORITY   159

NOTES   183

INDEX   197

■

Religious experience, in other words, spontaneously and
inevitably engenders myths, superstitions, dogmas, creeds,
and metaphysical theologies, and criticisms of one set of
these by the adherents of another.
—William James

No people at the present day can be explained by their
national religion.
—Emerson

INTRODUCTION:
SPIRITUAL POLITICS

I F, at the end of World War II, a commentator on American religion had predicted that in the course of the next forty years urban mass revivalism would be rekindled; a Roman Catholic politician would be elected president and Roman Catholic priests convicted of destroying draft files; a German-Jewish immigrant would become Secretary of State; untold numbers of Americans would attach themselves to Oriental gurus and self-help cults; the birthday of a Negro minister would become a national holiday; prayer would be banned from public schools and the teaching of Darwinian evolution embroiled in controversy; a fundamentalist account of the Millennium would be the best-selling book of one decade and fundamentalist ministers the best-known leaders of American Protestantism in the next; then he (or she) would likely have been dismissed as the prisoner of a bizarre, if obscure, fantasy. That all this has actually come to pass may suggest, among other things, a growing toleration of religious differences, the persistence of religious experimentation, the coming of age of Roman Catholicism, the revival of evangelical Protestantism as a national force. But can these oddly assorted phenomena be said to signify something about American religion *as a whole?* Is there, in any useful sense, such a thing?

When Emerson asserted that "no people at the present day can be explained by their national religion," he seemed to be thinking only of peoples possessed of a formal ecclesiastical establishment: the claim, opening the essay "Religion" in *English Traits*, introduces a discussion of that spiritual dead weight of British life, the Church of England. Yet, in his sly way, Emerson went ahead and used this same national religion to explain a good deal about the English: their conservatism, their class structure, their materialism. Americans, of course, had no established church; as Emerson put it elsewhere, " 'Tis as flat anarchy in our ecclesiastic realms as that which existed in Massachusetts in the Revolution, or which prevails now on the slope of the Rocky Mountains or Pike's Peak." The sober old faiths had collapsed, and no one was in charge: "witness the heathenisms in Christianity, the periodic 'revivals,' the Millennium mathematics, the peacock ritualism, the retrogression to Popery, the maundering of Mormons, the squalor of Mesmerism, the deliration of rappings, the rat and mouse revelation, thumps in table-drawers, and black art." Could *this* stuff, the evident consequence of having no national religion, "explain" the American people?[1]

The anarchy which Emerson saw in the middle of the nineteenth century looks in retrospect like the heyday of national religious consensus. Catholics there were, and a few Jews and others, but the country was overwhelmingly Protestant; on the streets and in the schools, what the Reformation had wrought was taken for granted as the prevailing form of American faith; and the prevailing form of Protantism was the evangelical. The revivals which had first spread through the colonies during the Great Awakening of the 1730s and 1740s had established the basic rhythm of American spiritual life: an emphasis on religious experience over religious instruction, with moments of enthusiasm and periods of backsliding following each other in unending sequence. By the Civil War, the flames of revival had burst out so often that the territory along the Erie Canal, that great highway into the

American heartland, had come to be known as the Burnt-Over District. Whatever the views of Unitarian Boston and Transcendentalist Concord, the Methodists and Baptists (and Presbyterians and Congregationalists) in the rest of the country constituted a united evangelical front which dominated American religious life. Those who, nowadays, lament the spiritual disarray of American life might do well to ponder Emerson's assessment. It could happen that late-twentieth-century America will one day stand as someone else's Eden of unified, thriving faith.

By the numbers, certainly, religion has been a big success in contemporary America. Church membership broke the 60-percent mark in the mid-1950s, and thirty years later it remains in that territory; poll after poll registers only small percentages of Americans who disbelieve in God or lack a religious identification. But if religion seems to enlist the support of more Americans than ever, one can question, and many have, what the numbers really mean. How does joining, say, the Methodist church down the block today compare with being accepted into a church in Puritan New England, which was supposed to signify membership in the communion of visible saints? Is it no more than a cultural taboo against confessing unbelief that obliges Americans to insist to pollsters that God and the Bible mean something to them? And what of the relative absence of religion in the central arteries of our culture—in our textbooks and general-circulation magazines, on network television, in literature and art? What of secularism?

In the mid-fifties, Will Herberg noted that while four-fifths of Americans said they believed the Bible to be the "revealed word of God" rather than merely a "great work of literature," only 53 percent could name so much as a single one of the Gospels. For him, this was a sign of how skin-deep most Americans' faith was. But skin-deep in comparison with what? In a recent study of Lutheran education in Germany after the Reformation, Gerald Strauss showed that for all the reformers' determination to bring religious knowledge to ordinary people, German Lutherans of the year 1600 were no better able to answer questions about the Christian faith than were the post-war Americans who supplied Herberg's polling data. Should this be taken to imply that ordinary people have never been very religious? Or that they have ordinarily been ignorant of the faith they profess? Or that tests of religious knowledge disclose little about depths of religious commitment?

The more we hold them up for scrutiny, the more tortuous such questions become. They are not, however, the only questions that can be asked of religion "as a whole" in a society; and they are not the questions with which this book is primarily concerned. Piety, how and to what degree people practice and profess their faith, I leave to students of particular groups and denominations. But neither is my primary concern with issues of church and state—with school prayer, aid to parochial schools, conscientious objection, public proselytizing, municipal crèches, and so on, all of which turn on interpretations of the First Amendment's joint prohibition of an establishment of religion and of interference in the free exercise thereof.

Instead, the focus here will be on attitudes and impulses and ideas, expressed in word and deed, that convey what people have taken to be the place and purpose of religion in their society. For though Americans may have decided to forgo a national religion, they do not lack a spiritual politics; nor does this politics represent some small action taking place in a remote theater of the nation's life. Whatever one thinks of it, religion remains an integral part of the American cultural system; for good or ill, it is one of the principal means by which Americans conduct their cultural business. Notwithstanding the awesome variety of religious belief and behavior in the United States, there does exist a distinctive religious dynamic which is bound up with, and makes manifest, what the country is undergoing at any given time. The purpose of this book is to show how that dynamic has operated in the years since World War II.

In 1977, the distinguished American church historian Sidney Mead wrote of "an unresolved intellectual tension between the theology professed and promulgated by a majority of the sects, and the theology that legitimates the institutional structures of the American democratic way and style of life." At bottom, this tension was between exclusivist creeds and a spiritually inclusive national faith. How is democracy possible when one is constrained to regard most or many of one's fellow citizens as reprobate, or at least outside the fellowship of the faithful? How is sectarianism possible when one is constrained to regard all as equally deserving members of the community? As the economist Kenneth Boulding likes to say, whatever exists is possible; and somehow Americans have managed to muddle along with their double vision. In Mead's view, the "theology" of the state had in fact won out, but at a real cost to both "theologies."[2] Whether or not one agrees with that conclusion, the tension itself should not be glossed over. It is the dilemma of pluralism, the central religious issue of our time.

The most important Western experiment in religious pluralism prior to our own occurred within the Roman Empire. But the reason that a great variety of religious beliefs and practices could coexist in relative harmony under Roman rule was that nearly all were nonexclusive. An individual could belong to many cults and sects without offending any one of them; religious practice was additive, syncretistic. Nor was "church" separate from the Roman state, which secured its own sacral position through a variety of liturgies. The late historian of ancient religion Arthur Darby Nock called this associative style of religious identification "adhesion." Adhesion, however, was impossible in two cases: Judaism and Christianity. These were faiths that demanded exclusive commitment from their devotees, insisting that there be no dabbling in other religious activity, be that the medical cult of the God Asclepius or the perfunctory rites entailed in paying respect to the emperor. An outsider who wanted to join these anomalous faiths had to convert; this signaled (in Nock's words) a "deliberate turning from indifference or from an earlier form of piety to another, a turning which implies a consciousness that a great change is involved, that the old was wrong and the new is right."[3] It was Christianity which, through its determined evangelism, became the conversion religion par excellence.

And when Christianity triumphed, it imposed its exclusivism on the state, bringing Roman religious pluralism to an end. Toleration of other beliefs was simply toleration of error.

The United States, like the rest of the West, is heir to the exclusivism of the conversion religions; its spectacular religious diversity results precisely from the historical tendency of such faiths to divide and subdivide into additional, mutually hostile bodies which are, in principle anyway, equally separated from the government. Yet American society is also subject to powerful *adhesional* impulses—the desire for a common religious cause as well as for a quasi-spiritual allegiance to the religiously impartial state. In America, a church signifies at once an exclusivist body standing for itself alone, and one among many such institutions serving the public weal.

Conversion and adhesion have been entwined throughout the nation's history. To found a country where people could worship according to the dictates of their conscience was to incarnate, profoundly, a Protestant principle; and many Protestants had little trouble enlisting under the banner of adhesional Americanism. During the revolutionary period, the most millenarian of rhetoric was made to serve the cause of national independence. In the postrevolutionary age of the "Second Great Awakening"—when evangelical Protestantism established its hegemony over American culture—small sects, utopian communities, even new religions (like Mormonism) proliferated, bearing witness to a conversional style anxious to close itself off from the culture at large. The stronger challenge to adhesion came later in the century, with the large-scale immigration of Roman Catholics and Jews. Not that the Catholics and Jews felt hostile to their new country. But Catholicism in particular—"popery"—had long been regarded as antipathetic to the democratic spirit of America; in the face of often virulent prejudice, the Catholics set up their own schools, retreating into their own ecclesiastical subculture in many parts of the country. Jews were likewise made to feel less than full partners in building the New World Zion.

The leading Protestant churches came to feel that what

divided them from each other mattered less than what divided them from these others, and a powerful spirit of pan-Protestant enterprise took hold—a Third Great Awakening, in the view of some. Efforts were mounted to Protestantize the cities, where the teeming immigrant populations lived. Nor did the spirit flag at the water's edge. The Student Volunteer Movement, founded in 1888, mobilized the largest missionary force in history with its slogan "the evangelization of the world in this generation." In 1908 the Federal Council of Churches was established, linking the denominations of mainline Protestantism in pursuit of the reformist goals of the new Social Gospel. And twelve years later, the century-long Protestant campaign against the evils of alcohol triumphed in the final ratification of the Eighteenth Amendment.

After these successes—and with the flow of non-Protestants into the country stanched by World War I and postwar immigration legislation—the 1920s promised halcyon times for adhesional faith, Protestant style. As the churches pushed their program of "Christian Americanization," an advertising man named Bruce Barton portrayed Jesus as the outdoorsy, sociable "founder of modern business" in The Man Nobody Knows, the decade's best-selling book. Then, in 1925, the Scopes "monkey trial" marked the turning point in the long-simmering conflict between modernism and fundamentalism in Protestant America. Presbyterian and Northern Baptist fundamentalists, who had threatened to take over their denominations, found themselves cast beyond the pale of civilization, their beliefs derided as part of the folkways of those "upland primates" about whom H. L. Mencken had written with such relish from Dayton, Tennessee.

Yet the would-be Protestant center would not hold. The 1928 presidential campaign of the Roman Catholic governor of New York, Al Smith, made clear not only that American nativism could be as ugly as ever, but also that non-Protestants would not consent to come placidly into the fold. Secular intellectuals, inspired with Marx, Freud, and positivistic science, challenged the churches' role as primary mediators of culture to the masses. As for the Depression, while the fundamentalists survived and prospered in the backwaters of American culture and "sects" like Jehovah's Witnesses grew apace, it brought no religious revival to the tents of mainline Protestantism. The missionary impulse itself faltered as liberals wondered what business they had pushing their spiritual wares on an ungrateful world. Jesus the first M.B.A.? New theological winds were blowing through the seminaries which called into question the Christ of American culture, and the Christ of the state as well. Clerical enthusiasm for World War I, thoroughly castigated in Roy Abrams' well-received 1933 study *Preachers Present Arms,* was now something to be ashamed of; one survey put 60 percent of American clergymen on record against war. It took Pearl Harbor to restore their identification with the armed forces.

As preachers from all but the pacifist faiths presented themselves for the military chaplaincy, there was every reason to wonder what spiritual politics the latest world war would leave in its wake. Could this new sense of common purpose be sustained? Might the old religious optimism be restored? Would Protestantism regain its lost sense of being the national religion, and if not, was there anything that could take its place?[4] And what of those humane values in whose name this best of all fights was being fought? Would final victory also signify a triumph for them?

▪ THE AGE OF ANXIETY

O N August 9, 1945, the day after the devastation of Nagasaki, a complaint came down from the Federal Council of Churches, high citadel of America's Protestant establishment, over the signatures of G. Bromley Oxnam, its president, and John Foster Dulles, the prominent international lawyer and Presbyterian layman who ran its Commission on a Just and Durable Peace. Having stipulated that the United States had just perpetrated mass destruction on an unimagined scale, the two stated that if "we, a professedly Christian nation, feel morally free to use atomic energy in that way, men elsewhere will accept that verdict. Atomic weapons will be looked upon as a normal part of the arsenal of war and the stage will be set for the sudden and final destruction of mankind. . . . We pray that our authorities may, in this difficult matter, find and follow the way of Christian statesmanship."[1] The meaning was clear enough: immediately cease and desist from dropping atomic bombs on Japanese cities.

As it happened, there were no more atomic bombs on hand to drop, but Harry Truman did not mention the fact in his handwritten response. No one, he wrote, was more disturbed by the use of the bomb than he, but he was also disturbed by the bombing of Pearl Harbor and the Japanese murder of American prisoners of war. "When you have to deal with a beast you have to treat him as a beast. It is most regrettable but nevertheless true." This may not have been the response Oxnam and Dulles were looking for, yet they were prepared to let inaction speak louder than words. After the Japanese surrender, they gave thanks that peace had been achieved without further recourse to atomic weaponry, and allowed, with a conditioned phrase, that the way of Christian statesmanship had more or less been found: "To the extent that our nation followed that way, it showed a capacity of self restraint which greatly increased our moral authority in the world."[2]

But not all Protestant protests were so easily stilled. *The Christian Century*, the establishment's undenominational voice, editorialized on August 15 that instead of indulging in self-congratulation, "we should now be standing in penitence before the Creator of the power which the atom has hitherto kept inviolate, using what may be our last opportunity to learn the lost secret of peace on earth." A few days later, a group of thirty-four clergymen denounced the bomb as "an atrocity of a new magnitude," stating that its "reckless and irresponsible employment against an already virtually beaten foe will have to receive judgment before God and the conscience of humankind. It has our unmitigated condemnation." They called on President Truman to discontinue production of atomic bombs and to seek international agreements outlawing not only the new weapon but war itself. Heading the list of petitioners were John Haynes Holmes of the War Resisters League and A. J. Muste of the Fellowship of Reconciliation: this was the voice of American pacifism. While few other Protestant spokesmen or editorialists went so far, criticism and concern were sufficiently widespread for one well-placed observer to have anticipated "serious tension" between the churches and the American government, had the war gone on much longer. In the event, the Federal Council decided to request a report on atomic warfare from its Commission on the Relation of the

Church to the War in the Light of the Christian Faith. The chairman was Professor Robert L. Calhoun of Yale, one of the signers of the Holmes-Muste appeal.[3]

Among those sitting on the Calhoun Commission were Reinhold Niebuhr, John Bennett, and Henry P. Van Dusen, leading antipacifist theologians who before the war had made the case for U.S. intervention. Yet the commission report, which came out in March of 1946, took nearly as hard a line as had the pacifists by themselves. "We are agreed that, whatever be one's judgment of the ethics of war in principle, the surprise bombing of Hiroshima and Nagasaki is morally indefensible." It had been done without specific warning or prior demonstration, and had not been necessary for victory. "As the power that first used the atomic bomb under these circumstances, we have sinned grievously against the laws of God and the people of Japan." The commission, in addition, felt compelled to reconsider its earlier approval of the saturation bombing of German and Japanese cities. The bombs of August were simply part of the "whole system of obliteration attacks with explosives and firebombs"; both kinds of "indiscriminate, excessive violence" had to be condemned.[4] Such readiness to condemn was a natural outgrowth of the Protestant determination, during the war, to preserve some moral perspective on U.S. warmaking, the new weapon brought prewar clerical pacifists and their interventionist opponents together in a common cause.

By contrast, the leaders of Roman Catholicism mixed their signals. Two days after Hiroshima, the Pope's press office was quoted as saying that the "use of atomic bombs in Japan has created an unfavorable impression on the Vatican"; and wide coverage was given to L'Osservatore Romano's August 7 editorial, which pointedly contrasted the inventors of the new weapon with Leonardo da Vinci, who was supposed to have done away with his plans for a submarine lest they be used to create an instrument of destruction. A day later, however, official spokesmen were at pains to deny that Rome "as such" had taken a stand—although they granted that "among the hundreds of priests in the Vatican a feeling of deep personal revulsion against the use of so awesome a weapon has welled up." Neither did the American Catholic bishops, in the manner of a later day, decry with one public voice; the archbishop of New York, Francis Spellman, saw to that. As ordinary, or chief Catholic chaplain, of the U.S. military, Spellman remained unshakably supportive of American warmaking throughout his long term in office. Yet while Rome and the American hierarchy refrained from official comment, the Catholic opinion that *was* expressed amounted to a chorus of hostility unmatched in any other religious body.[5]

From leading periodicals like *Catholic World* and *Commonweal* to such diverse figures as Archbishop Richard Cushing of Boston, radio celebrity Fulton Sheen, and Dorothy Day of the radical Catholic Worker movement, Catholic denunciation of the atomic bomb relied on Thomas Aquinas' theory of just war. Setting forth the grounds on which wars could legitimately be fought, just-war theory was considered part of natural law (God's eternal law as engraved in human nature), and was therefore binding on all human communities, Christian or otherwise. Wars, according to Aquinas, had to be fought not only for a just end but by just means as well; no object, however good or necessary, could justify recourse to evil. A sharp distinction between combatants and noncombatants needed to be drawn; the idea of total war, with an entire population seen as involved in the war effort and hence fair game, was rejected out of hand. Catholic writers had used these arguments to condemn Allied obliteration bombing, and they now applied them to the atomic bombing. It had been evil because it had destroyed combatants and noncombatants indiscriminately. The argument that a million American lives would otherwise have been lost in an invasion of Japan carried no moral weight.

Just-war theory also attracted some non-Catholics, among them Henry Luce, the emperor of Time, Inc. Though the good Presbyterian son of a great Presbyterian missionary, Luce was married to a famous Catholic convert and liked to talk religion with his friend the Jesuit theologian John Courtney Murray. In a 1948 address to the United Council of Church Women, he stated that all serious Christian thinking about war began with Thomist doctrine. Aquinas, he said, insisted that there had to be clearly defined objectives and conditions for a war to be just, and here the U.S. had fallen short. He himself had been with the fleet in the Pacific a few months before Hiroshima, and it had been evident both that the Japanese were beaten and that they were increasingly willing to quit. "If, instead of our doctrine of 'unconditional surrender,' we had all along made our conditions clear, I have little doubt that the war with Japan would have ended soon without the bomb explosion which so jarred the Christian conscience."[6]

Though Japanese willingness to surrender remains a matter of dispute, Luce was at least partly right: the Christian conscience had not been asleep at the birth of the atomic age. But what signified its being awake? The war, after all, had been a righteous one, and what was done was done. As a high official of the Federal Council wrote to A. J. Muste on September 5, 1945, it was now more important to work for effective international control of atomic energy than to "divide our forces" by dwelling on the evils of Hiroshima and Nagasaki.[7] Divided or not, the forces looking to dwell on the evils of Hiroshima and Nagasaki were supported by no groundswell of public opinion. Outright opposition to the dropping of the bomb was a bare 1.7 percent in the secular press, and the polls of George Gallup and Elmo Roper consistently showed 75 percent of the American people approving the action. The spiritual impact of the bomb must be sought beyond the religious spokesmen who explicitly condemned its use.

Within weeks of the war's end, a teacher at the Moody Bible Institute in Chicago, the country's leading fundamentalist seminary, outlined parallels between scriptural pronouncements on the Apocalypse and the reports on Hiroshima and Nagasaki, assuring his radio audience that before man set the world afire, "God Himself will do that which He here predicts He will do." Downstate, the editor of the Pekin Daily Times suggested that because our heads had developed beyond our hearts, the government should force all citizens to attend church schools five days a week. In the first of a series of annual essays on the new era, the old New Dealer Rexford Tugwell mused how Christianity "as a doctrine embedded in people's hearts" might have prepared the world for atomic power. ("Come to think of it, the wonder was that it had not.") Yet, he went on, it was just in our modern atmosphere that Christianity seemed to function less well.[8]

In "Morality for the Atomic Age," his *New Leader* column of September 8, 1945, Columbia professor Eduard C. Lindeman cast a querulous eye over the first batch of such pronouncements: "The main cry which has risen among the alarmists since the announcement of atomic energy's discovery may be epitomized as another 'back to religion' claim. This demand usually includes at least two hidden elements, namely (a) an assumption that morality resides in and may be evoked from no other source than religion, and (b) an assumption that there is something sinister about science. Some publicists have even gone so far as to make the ridiculous proposal that scientific activities be halted or curtailed until men bring religion and morals into a position of par." In the following months, the prominent social critic Lewis Mumford emerged in the first rank of those Lindeman had in mind. Early in 1946, Mumford, having already called for the destruction of all atomic weapons, published a Program for Survival which attacked the "dehumanized thinking" of the physical sciences. What was needed, he said, was fewer physical scientists and more social scientists, fewer schools of technology and more schools of humanities. And "not the least important force we must mobilize, in the interests of survival, is an ancient one: that of religion." All the great religions, he said, had sought to curb destructive impulses, encourage propagation, foster love. The function of religion, moreover, was to reduce conceit, complacence, and intellectual pride; with mankind "a-float on a frail life-raft," that was the preparation needed "to face the ordeal of reality."[9]

A similar line was taken by the former Trotskyite Dwight Macdonald, who was devoting his new journal *Politics* to the search for a new radicalism which would cut across left and

right but mostly oppose the Marxist Progressivism of his earlier days. In "The Root Is Man," a long essay which appeared
in April and July of 1946, Macdonald announced that the
atomic bomb had "leveled . . . the whole structure of Progressive assumptions on which liberal and socialist theory has
been built for two centuries." The course of history could no
longer be assumed to be leading to happiness and prosperity.
Science had proved incapable of generating the values that
humanity needed to survive. Those values—truth, love, and
justice—were absolute; absolute because they were ends in
themselves and possessed "an element which was not historically relative." Although he claimed no personal ties to religion, Macdonald wanted to admit religious people into the
radical fold. The "radical vision," he asserted, was religious,
"if by 'religious' is simply meant non-materialistic or non-
scientific." [10]

The bomb in fact revived a prewar intellectual debate over
"scientific naturalism," furnishing the opponents of a purely
naturalistic understanding of the universe with heavy new ar-
tillery. What clearer product of Einsteinian science than the
bomb? What scientific achievement more threatening to
human values? The large effort by a number of the bomb's
inventors to foster international control of atomic energy (embodied in the Bulletin of the Atomic Scientists) seemed less a
testimony to the morality of science than a belated admission
of its inadequacy. To Mumford it meant that "the greatest of
all the madmen" had "finally awakened." The acerbic essayist
Milton Mayer, who breathed the neo-Aristotelian air of the
University of Chicago, found instructive the "agony" of those
who, "when they saw what they had done, broke down and
wept." Their misfortune, he wrote, was that they had believed
the myth that as scientists they were working for humanity.
"They might have been useful men, instead of murderous me-
chanics, had they been Thomists instead of atomists." Prisoners of an educational system "sold out to the legend of
scientism," they had never encountered "the only area of understanding that men positively have to encounter, and early
in their days, in order to live a human life and build up a

human society: the area of the moral virtues." A true Thomist, of course, knew this only too well. "In a way," declared Francis X. Murphy in *Catholic World*, "the release of atomic energy is a symbol of what has happened to the libertarian world of yesterday. The physical destruction of Nagasaki and Hiroshima were well foreshadowed in the release of human fury at the breakdown of Christian moral ideals." (Paul Tillich was a bit less severe. "The attitude of the inventors of the atom bomb in the first months after its successful application," he wrote, "was a very impressive unity of scientific pride and moral despair.")[11]

The theme of scientism repentant before the bomb was most heavily treated in "Dedication Day," a black fable which appeared in the April, 1946, number of *Politics*. Its author, James Agee, was a protégé of Macdonald's who wrote features and film criticism for Time, Inc. In the story, a fabulous arch has been erected in the nation's capital to memorialize this "greatest of human achievements." The dedication ceremonies reflect American civic piety at its finest, complete with Boy Scout bugler, twenty-one-gun salute, doves wired with artificial olive branches, and Arturo Toscanini conducting the last movement of Beethoven's *Ninth Symphony*—all taking place under the beneficent gaze of representative Protestant, Catholic, and Jewish clergymen. But an incident mars the "otherwise perfect day." After attending Mass, visiting Quaker meetings, and even contemplating pilgrimage to Tibet, an atomic scientist has arranged to be the one to throw the switch on the arch's "Eternal Fuse"; and in the act of doing so he swallows poison. The suicide calls forth psychoanalytic explanations, sermons on the dangers of excessive scrupulousness, and a symposium on "The New New Failure of Nerve" (a reference to *Partisan Review*'s famous 1943 symposium, "The New Failure of Nerve," on an alleged religious revival among intellectuals). The story concludes with the repentant scientist transfigured into artifact: "our last link with a not-too-distant past in which such conceptions as those of 'atonement,' and 'guilt,' and 'individual responsibility,' still had significance." But Agee, who was himself responsible for *Time*'s apocalyptic cover story on Hiroshima, was not exactly a voice crying in the wilderness.

In a lecture to the University of Chicago's Channing Club in January of 1950, David Riesman pointed to a shift in power positions between science on one side and religion on the other. Science, he said, had become fair game, while religion was now beyond the reach of criticism in American society. Riesman, a follower of the dean of American secular liberalism, John Dewey, placed the blame on a new "united front" of religionists and intellectuals. A few months later, Partisan Review updated "The New Failure of Nerve" with "Religion and the Intellectuals," a multi-issue symposium which began with the editorial pronouncement that one of the most important developments of the time was "the new turn toward religion among intellectuals and the growing disfavor with which secular attitudes and perspectives are now regarded in not a few circles that lay claim to the leadership of culture." Where once the elimination of religion had been envisaged, "at present many thinkers sound an insistent note of warning that Western civilization cannot hope to survive without the re-animation of religious values." Sidney Hook, the moving force behind the earlier symposium, indicted "the spirit of fin du mondisme generated by the liberation of nuclear energy" for helping inspire the "tidal wave" of religious sentiment. John Dewey himself connected the "present loss of faith in science" to, again, a "loss of intellectual nerve." But from Agee (who led things off) and Macdonald, to the poets Allen Tate, R. P. Blackmur, and W. H. Auden, to the theologians Paul Tillich and Jacques Maritain, religion more than held its own in the pages of Partisan Review. Admittedly, many of the proreligion intellectuals declined to avow a specific creed. It had become good form, sneered the art critic Meyer Schapiro, to "appreciate" religion without believing in God or accepting the discipline of a church. "Religion," he said, "now has its fellow-travelers." The question, however, was why.[12]

In the postwar period, an appreciation of religion became the vehicle which took the intellectuals away from that central article of modern faith, the idea of progress. For if the radicalism of the thirties had still been animated by a "progressive" desire to remake the world, the accumulated chastisements meted out to civilization by the twentieth century now demanded a humbler view of man and his works. Human imperfectibility, the blurring of good and evil, the ironic failures of attempted reform, the perils of utopianism: these were the hallmarks of a new counterprogressive outlook. Søren Kierkegaard replaced John Dewey as the philosopher of the modern condition. Reinhold Niebuhr, the author of *Moral Man and Immoral Society*, came into his own as America's premier political theologian. George Orwell, bringing out *Nineteen Eighty-four* in 1949, assumed the prophet's mantle. The suicide of "Dedication Day" was, *in fine*, a type of the new existentialist hero, bearing angst-ridden moral witness in a depraved and uncomprehending universe. When W. H. Auden's *The Age of Anxiety* appeared in 1947, the title of a dramatic poem about the temper of wartime was immediately seized upon to christen the postwar era. And so, for the intellectuals, it seemed to be. But what of all the others? Was it also an age of anxiety for them?

From the beginning it had been made clear to the American public that the splitting of the atom had hung human existence in the balance. The day after Hiroshima, CBS Radio's "Service to the Front" program presented a dramatization of the development and first use of atomic power, and at its conclusion a nationwide audience heard the narrator solemnly intone, "Tonight we know surely and forever that the choice is good will and human brotherhood—or the end of all things on earth." If World War I had been fought to make the world safe for democracy, World War II had evidently succeeded in making the world safe for nothing at all. The popular press was soon filled with predictions that other nations, including ones not friendly to the United States, would soon develop atomic bombs of their own, and that given the experience of aerial bombardment during the war, no military defense against a determined atomic attack was possible.

In September of 1945, Joseph and Stewart Alsop laid out a doomsday scenario ("Your Flesh Should Creep") for the readers of the *Saturday Evening Post*, basing their portrait of an atomically bombed America on a Pentagon study which concluded that the "only sure defense is now the political defense." A few months later, *Reader's Digest* ran a more localized atomic nightmare, "Mist of Death over New York," written by one of the Pentagon study's authors, Lt. Col. David Parker. Everything in our power, wrote Parker, had to be done to ensure international control of atomic energy. In a November, 1945, press release, George Gallup's American Institute of Public Opinion announced that questions about atomic bombs and atomic energy had proved to be "of overwhelmingly greater interest to the people of the United States than any other issue on the ballot"; never before had it found "such continuous public interest in one particular subject or issue."

A Roper Poll conducted late in 1945 discovered that 65.6 percent of Americans expected another country to have the bomb within five years; 40.4 percent believed that country would be Russia; 38 percent anticipated a "big war" sometime in the next twenty-five to thirty years. In the summer of 1946, the Social Science Research Council undertook a series of extensive and intensive surveys of public reaction to the atomic bomb. Nearly half of those who filled out the questionnaires for the extensive survey considered that a world war was either in the cards or possible in the next quarter-century, and nearly two-thirds thought there was a "real danger" that atomic bombs would at some point be dropped on the United States. Only one-fourth of those intensively surveyed said the bomb had them worried, as against over 60 percent who said it did not. But of the 79 percent who gave reasons for a lack of worry, a scant 3 percent cited the belief that an effective military defense would be developed. Two-thirds of them indicated that worrying was useless because individuals were helpless to do anything about the atomic danger.

The worry that registered most clearly after the war was of the useful kind people thought they could do something about. March, 1946, saw the publication of *Peace of Mind*, a volume of spiritual self-help by a Reform rabbi named Joshua Loth Liebman. "If ever there was a timely book, this is it," wrote the pacifist John Haynes Holmes in the *New York Herald Tribune.* "To a distressed and despairing generation, beset by confusion, tortured by fears, the brilliant Rabbi of Temple Israel, Boston, comes with his balm of spiritual healing." The balm was not meant to anesthetize. Some worries, including fear of the bomb, Liebman held real and necessary; what he sought to cure were the unreal and unnecessary—the neurotic—ones. His formula was a compound of Freudian psychology and liberal religion. "Thou shalt not be afraid of thy hidden impulses" was the first of his "commandments of a new morality." Atheism was largely a matter of childhood frustration, adolescent disillusionment, and adult feelings of intellectual inferiority. By facing up to private feelings of guilt and distress, "a new birth of confidence in life and in the God of life" could be achieved: "How overwhelmingly the similarities between religion and psychiatry heap up at the end of our quest for inward peace!" It was a quest that Americans were happy to buy into; the book was number two nonfiction bestseller in 1946, number one in 1947, and number three in 1948.[13]

By 1948 Liebman had competition in the inner-peace market: *How to Stop Worrying and Start Living* by the master of winning friends and influencing people, Dale Carnegie, and *A Guide to Confident Living* by the Reverend Norman Vincent Peale. Peale, pastor of the Marble Collegiate Church on New York's Fifth Avenue, quickly established himself as the country's leading apostle of Mind Cure, or, as Peale entitled his next book, The Power of Positive Thinking. This therapeutic faith proposed that psychological, physical, and material difficulties derived less from hostile outside forces (though the world *was* a threatening place) than from the wrong mental attitude. Changing the latter would make all the difference. Health, wealth, and happiness were accessible through a kind of autosuggestive prayer aimed at drawing upon the limitless supply of divine power. "The most powerful form of energy one can generate," *Confident Living* confidently asserted, "is not mechanical, electronic or even atomic energy, but prayer energy."[14] The cured mind, so empowered, need fear nothing.

Did the quasi-religious pursuit of peace of mind and confident living—an end to worry—have anything to do with The
Bomb? In 1951, George S. Stevenson, psychiatrist and medical
director of the National Commission for Mental Hygiene, proposed psychotherapy as a partial antidote for the "atomic jitters" that he saw sweeping the country. Let us suppose that
Americans internalized some atomic unease—and perhaps
some atomic guilt—in the form of more private distresses; and
that Liebman and company were the psychotherapists they
turned to for help. Still: Mind Cure had been calming frazzled
middle-class American nerves ever since Mary Baker Eddy
founded Christian Science late in the nineteenth century; Carnegie and Peale, with their promises of material success, were
in a position to tap into widely expressed fears of renewed
economic depression just after the war; and the Red Scare of
1919 showed that a postwar America did not need to meditate
on the atom in order to feel jittery about Communism. All that
can be said with certainty is that the need for some kind of
religious rescue from anxiety became a popular message in the
late forties, filtering the debates and laments of the intellectuals into the general culture.[15]

Science was not the enemy, insisted the French émigré
physiologist Pierre Lecompte du Noüy in his best-seller of
1947, Human Destiny. But scientific civilization, the latest
step on the ladder of evolutionary progress, needed a spiritual
leash. "We know that intelligence can turn against itself and
destroy man unless it is controlled by a moral force." That
force was contained in the Christian religion. Man had the
choice, either to disregard the divine spark in his nature "or to
come closer to God by showing his eagerness to work with
Him, and for Him." A grimmer evangel was conveyed in another 1947 best-seller, the pointedly updated abridgment of
the first six volumes of Arnold Toynbee's A Study of History.
According to Toynbee's historical metaphysics, two world
wars and the atomic bomb provided good reason to think that
Western civilization was succumbing, like the twenty-five civ-
ilizations that had preceded it, to forces of disintegration.
"This swift succession of catastrophic events on a steeply

mounting gradient inevitably inspires a dark doubt about our future, and this doubt threatens to undermine our faith and hope at a critical eleventh hour which calls for the utmost exertion of these saving spiritual faculties. Here is a challenge which we cannot evade, and our destiny depends on our response." For the correct response, Toynbee advised taking a leaf from John Bunyan's seventeenth-century spiritual allegory *Pilgrim's Progress*. Its hero, Christian, at *his* eleventh hour, avoided Death in the City of Destruction not through his own devices but by encountering The Evangelist. We, for our part, "may and must pray that a reprieve which God has granted to our society once will not be refused if we ask for it again in a humble spirit and with a contrite heart." The West would survive, in Toynbee's view, if Westerners turned to God.[16]

Catholic writers did not stint on more up-to-date allegories. In early 1947, for example, Clare Boothe Luce took to the pages of *McCall's* to tell the story of her own conversion to the Roman church. The onetime actress and playwright, now Republican congresswoman from Connecticut and mistress of Time, Inc., declared that Liberalism, Humanitarianism, and Communism, which had all commanded her sympathies before the war, were all expressions of a world that had tried to get along without God. It was a world where tyrants not only went unpunished, but were also barely distinguishable from liberators and saviors. "For what, above all, is the answer to the question raised by the slaughter of the innocents, by our side, in many a bombing raid? And what about the thousands who were slain at Hiroshima? Who shall avenge the 'avenged' and who judge the judges, O moderns? Do the dead children of Hiroshima ask wiser questions than atomic scientists can answer?" For her, the real conflict was between the forces of modern thought and the forces of belief. The emblem of modernity was the atomic bomb, whose devotees professed the *anticredo* of an antireligion:

> Let us pray! (In the First Church of Atomic Fission): "I believe in the Atom, Power Almighty, Substance of Heaven and Earth, once and forever divisible, first split at Oak Ridge, as

prophesied by St. Einstein, then dropped over Hiroshima in the form of a bomb, killing millions, still to be split over the whole world, whence it may bring the atomic Kingdom of Heaven on Earth; or come to judge mankind obsolete. I believe in Uranium, Plutonium and the Cyclotron; the Communion of Scientists; the corruption of the body; the relativity of all mind and matter, world with an end, Amen."

Where, she demanded, could one find priests who would protest that God was Love, that the uses to which man put atomic energy would depend solely on whether he worshiped the God of Love? "I find such priests now very often in Catholic Churches."[17]

In the same vein, Fulton Sheen's *Peace of Soul*, a *Peace of Mind* competitor that hit the best-seller list in 1949, began by pointing out that in the hands of a Francis of Assisi the atomic bomb would be less harmful than a pistol in the hands of a thug; its danger lay not in the energy it contained but in the man who used it. It was necessary, therefore, to remake modern man, who would likely harm the planet itself "unless he can stop the explosions inside his own mind." Only through conversion to Catholicism would "anxiety, the grave complaint of imprisoned modern man," give way to true inner peace.[18] For illustration, Sheen had merely to point a few notches up the list of best-selling nonfiction, to Thomas Merton's *The Seven Storey Mountain*; in fact, his own testimonial could be found on the book's dust jacket: "a Twentieth Century form of the Confessions of St. Augustine."

It was the spiritual autobiography of a sensitive young man with literary ambitions. Like Augustine carousing his student days away in fourth-century Carthage, Merton had given himself over to such physical and intellectual debaucheries as New York offered a Columbia undergraduate in the 1930s: wine, women, and some Communist fellow-traveling. "I had refused to pay any attention to the moral laws upon which all our vitality and sanity depend. . . . I had at last become a true child of the modern world. . . . In devouring pleasures and joys, I had found distress and anguish and fear."[19] A longing for religion, together with a discovery of medieval literature and philosophy, led him first to convert to Catholicism and then, on the medieval model, to leave the world altogether and become a monk. "The Christians are right; the pagans are wrong," pronounced the eleventh-century *Song of Roland.* Merton voiced a similar battle cry for Catholicism triumphant, but his book contained themes which non-Catholics too had learned to appreciate. There were dithyrambs in praise of the unities of medieval culture and the solid structure of scholastic morality—even kind words for the secular Thomism of the University of Chicago. The title referred to the seven levels of Dante's Purgatory: here was another intellectual journey up from the thirties, this time with an exotic Trappist twist.

"The religious revival confronting us is . . . primarily a literary tour-de-force" having "very little to do with American life as a whole," wrote *Partisan Review*'s editor William Phillips in his contribution to the "Religion and the Intellectuals" symposium.[20] Literary it surely was, even for those who had never heard of T. S. Eliot's *Four Quartets.* Among the most popular novels of the years 1947–52 were Russell Janney's *The Miracle of the Bells; The Bishop's Mantle* and *The Gown of Glory* by Agnes Sligh Turnbull; *Mary* and *Moses* by Sholem Asch; Henry Morton Robinson's *The Cardinal;* Thomas Costain's *The Chalice;* Giovanni Guareschi's *Don Camillo and His Flock;* and *The Foundling,* by His Eminence himself, Archbishop Spellman. At least in the books they read, ordinary Americans seemed to be looking in God's direction for help with what ailed them.

But what of "American life as a whole"? It did not take long for a statistical pattern to emerge. After the war, new churches began going up in unprecedented numbers. Funds spent on their construction rose from $26 million in 1945 to $76 million in 1946, $251 million in 1948, and $409 million in 1950; in 1960, the annual expenditure passed the $1-billion mark. Church membership as a percentage of total population was calculated to have grown 8 percent between 1940 and 1950, more than in the three previous decades combined; in the next decade it grew an additional fourteen points, from 55

THE AGE OF ANXIETY

to 69 percent. In 1960, one student of American religion announced that the postwar period had witnessed America's "Fourth Great Awakening."[21] Nor did this Awakening lack an adhesional identity.

2 ■ A NEW CREED

I N 1952, Modern Library brought out an edition of *What Makes Sammy Run?*, Budd Schulberg's 1941 best-seller about an unsavory Jewish immigrant son who claws his way in record time from the Lower East Side to the top of the movie industry. In a freshly written introduction, Schulberg offered a solution to the riddle of Sammy Glick: "In throwing over the ways of his father without learning any sense of obligation to the Judeo-Christian-democratic pattern, he had nothing except naked self-interest to guide himself." The same year, a few days before Christmas, President-elect Eisenhower gave a speech before the Freedoms Foundation in New York in which he called attention to the foundations of democracy. "Our form of government," he explained, "has no sense unless it is founded in a deeply felt religious faith, and I don't care what it is. With us of course it is the Judeo-Christian concept but it must be a religion that all men are created equal." As of 1952, good Americans were supposed to be good Judeo-Christians. It was the new national creed.[1]

In the beginning, "Judeo-Christian" had simply designated possible connections between Judaism and Christianity in ancient times. The term's first appearance, according to the Supplement to the *Oxford English Dictionary*, was in the *Literary Guide* in 1899: a "Judaeo-Christian 'continuity' theory" postulated the development of Church ritual out of the practices of the Second Temple. Not until some decades later did it begin to be used to refer to values or beliefs shared by Jews and Christians, to a common Western religious outlook. Writing in 1934, the American Communist Joseph Freeman spoke of "Judeo-Christian asceticism" and of seeing "Greek paganism . . . through Judeo-Christian spectacles." George Orwell, in a 1939 book review, remarked that not acting meanly was "a thing that carries no weight in the Judaeo-Christian scheme of morals." The dates and the politics of the authors are significant, for what brought this usage into regular discourse was opposition to fascism. Fascist fellow travelers and anti-Semites had appropriated "Christian" as a trademark; besides Father Coughlin's well-known Christian Front, there were such organizations as the Christian American Crusade, Christian Aryan Syndicate, Christian Mobilizers, and Christian Party, and publications like the *Christian Defender* and *Christian Free Press*. "Judeo-Christian" thus became a catchword for the other side. In its 1941 handbook, *Protestants Answer Anti-Semitism*, the left-liberal *Protestant Digest* described itself (for the first time) as "a periodical serving the democratic ideal which is implicit in the Judeo-Christian tradition."[2]

In his introduction to a 1942 volume of essays on anti-Semitism, Carl Friedrich, a Harvard government professor who had himself emigrated from Nazi Germany, asserted that the Jews might "well perish unless the Gentile world comes to see in truer perspective the vital part the Jews constitute in the total pattern of Judaeo-Christian world culture." But, he went on to ask, "what justifies the expression Judaeo-Christian culture? Are not Judaism and Christianity fundamentally opposed to each other?" The answer was no. Friedrich cited the French Catholic philosopher Jacques Maritain, who in *A Christian Looks at the Jewish Question* (1939) had advanced the "highly persuasive" proposition that in striking at the Jews anti-Semites were striking at Christ and Christianity. Maritain, whose wife, Raïssa, came from a Russian-Jewish family, himself wrote an essay while in the United States in 1942 in which he praised "la tradition judéo-chrétienne" as a source of the West's enduring values.[3]

Antifascist affirmation of a shared religious basis for Western values was nowhere more evident than at the large annual convocations of liberal academics and intellectuals known as the Conference on Science, Philosophy and Religion in Their Relation to the Democratic Way of Life, Inc. Organized in 1940 by Lyman Bryson of the Columbia Teachers College and Louis Finkelstein of the Jewish Theological Seminary, the Conference originated, in Professor Friedrich's words, "essentially as a rallying point for Judeo-Christian forces in America against the threat presented to them by the Axis ideology and actions." During the war and in the years immediately after it, participants denoted the spiritual underpinnings of democracy with "Judeo-Christian" and a family of related terms: "Hebraic-Christian," "Hebrew-Christian," "Jewish-Christian," "Judeo-Christianity," even "Judaistic-Christian." ("Totalitarianism is the historical result of the weakening of the Greek and Hebraic-Christian tradition we have described." "Tyranny can never tolerate the cultivation of the Hebrew-Christian tradition." Beneath all other contributing factors . . . modern democracy is rooted in the Hebrew Christian heritage of faith in God." "To deal effectively with the present crisis of civilization we must recognize that most of the cherished ideals are rooted unseverably in the Jewish-Christian faith.") The Judeo-Christian forces were not always precise about the meaning of their rallying cry. As Harvard's Douglas Bush commented after a particularly high-flown talk by the theologian Amos Wilder, "One could wish for fuller hints of what the Hebraic-Christian tradition, to which all pay at least vague lip service, actually does or can mean in modern terms for modern men of good will." Yet greater precision might have provoked unwanted disagreement when the idea was to invoke a common faith for a united democratic front. And Bush notwithstanding, not everyone concerned with the fate of the West was prepared to leap onto the Judeo-Christian bandwagon.[4]

Partisan Review's 1943 "failure of nerve" symposium was in fact a kind of antisymposium to the Conference on Science, Philosophy and Religion. Leading off, Sidney Hook, John Dewey, and Ernest Nagel all indicted the Conference for hostility to scientific naturalism, and Hook specifically turned his heavy guns on the Conference's "Hebraic-Christian philosophy of democracy and culture." In his view, the idea that modern democracy derived from egalitarian religious dogma was logically invalid, historically false, and irrelevant to the war against Hitlerism. In making religion the cornerstone of civilization, the Conference had, he insisted, traded in reason for the supernatural.[5]

Judeo-Christian enthusiasm also came under fire from the Jewish publicist Trude Weiss-Rosmarin, who in 1943 issued a tract criticizing statements by the president of Reform Judaism's Hebrew Union College, Julian Morgenstern. Speaking in the dark days of the war, Morgenstern had called for a partnership between Judaism and Christianity.

> Today we realize, as never since Christianity's birth, how intimate are the relations of the two religions, so intimate and insoluble that they are truly, basically one, that they have a common descent, a common vision, hope, mission, face a common foe and a common fate, must achieve a common victory or share a common death. We speak now, with still inadequate but steadily expanding understanding, of the Judeo-Christian heritage. We comprehend, as we have not comprehended in all of nineteen hundred years, that Judaism and Christianity are partners in the great work of world-redemption and the progressive unfolding of the world-spirit.

Separately, he said, each faith was unequal to the task; each had its own unique and necessary contribution to make "to what we may truthfully call Judaeo-Christianity, the religion of tomorrow's better world." This, to Weiss-Rosmarin, was dangerous nonsense. Judaism and Christianity were *not* basically one, and making Jewish–Christian goodwill depend on a shared religious identity was "a totalitarian aberration" fundamentally at odds with the pluralistic principles of democracy.[6]

But after the revelations of the Nazi death camps, a phrase like "our Christian civilization" began to seem ominously exclusive; greater comprehensiveness was needed for proclaiming the spirituality of the American Way. "When our own spiritual leaders look for the moral foundations for our democratic ideals," observed Cornell's Arthur E. Murphy at the 1949 Conference on Science, Philosophy and Religion, "it is in 'our Judeo-Christian heritage,' the culture of 'the West,' or 'the American tradition,' that they tend to find them." Murphy was contrasting America's spiritual leaders with the leaders of the Soviet Union, who proclaimed high-flying moral ideals of their own. So, for that matter, was President Eisenhower, who made his Judeo-Christian aside while describing the difficulty he once experienced explaining democracy to his favorite Soviet commander, Marshal Zhukov. ("And since at the age of 14 he had been taken over by the Bolshevik religion and had believed in it since that time, I was quite certain it was hopeless on my part to talk to him about the fact that our form of government is founded in religion.") At the National Federation of Temple Brotherhoods convention in October of 1951, Roger Straus, the federation's honorary president, declared that the "greatest peril" confronting the Western World was "the world-wide clash of two divergent beliefs: the Judeo-Christian philosophy and the crass materialism of communism." In July of the following year, at the convention of the Military Chaplains Association of the United States, Daniel Poling, the president of the association, warned, "We meet at a time when the Judeo-Christian faith is challenged as never before in all the years since Abraham left Ur of the Chaldees." Having proved itself against the Nazis, the Judeo-Christian tradition now did duty among the watchfires of the Cold War.[7]

Yet the hot and cold wars of mid-century did not alone account for the rise of the Judeo-Christian creed; there was a theological dimension as well. Since the late thirties, some American Protestant thinkers had begun to emphasize the ground that Christianity shared with Judaism. These were not, as might have been expected, liberal divines disposed to winnow Christian doctrine down to love of God and neighbor. Theirs, rather, was the darker vision of the Continental theology of crisis. They followed Karl Barth and Emil Brunner in scorning the optimistic image of man and his works that had prevailed in nineteenth-century Protestantism. The fundamental facts were man's sinfulness and his obligation to transform himself through faith in the absolute. Theology based on categories derived from ancient Greek and modern secular philosophy was denigrated in favor of a "biblical" theology that could better convey the personal relation between God and man pictured in Scripture.

In *The Challenge of Israel's Faith* (1944), the biblical scholar G. Ernest Wright attacked contemporary Protestantism for overconfident historicism in its approach to the Old Testament and undertook to sketch out the basic and enduringly relevant characteristics of Old Testament religion. Paul Minear of the Andover Newton Theological School took the same tack in *Eyes of Faith* (1946). Although both books expressed orthodox Christian beliefs, their aim was not the traditional apologetic one of showing the New Testament as fulfilling and superseding the Old. Instead, they sought to indicate the extent to which the New Testament belonged to the world of the Hebrew Bible, and to stress, against nineteenth-century theology, the centrality for Christianity of the Hebrew faith.

The foremost Christian "Hebraist" was none other than Reinhold Niebuhr. "I have, as a Christian theologian, sought to strengthen the Hebraic-prophetic content of the Christian tradition," wrote America's preeminent religious intellectual in 1944. In fact, Niebuhr's "neo-orthodox" conception of Christianity was then evolving increasingly toward the Hebraic. In the second volume of his 1939 Gifford lectures, revised and expanded for publication in 1943, he had stated, "The Christian belief that the meaning of both life and history is disclosed and fulfilled in Christ and his Cross, is in a sense a combination of Hellenic and Hebraic interpretations of life." Yet in *The Self and the Dramas of History* (1955), his last

major theological work, that was no longer the case: "The es-
sence of the Christian faith is drawn from the Hebraic, particularly the prophetic, interpretation of life and history, and is
erroneously interpreted as the consequence of a confluence of
Hebraic and Hellenic streams of thought."[8]

The distinction between the Hebraic and the Hellenic derived from the English poet and essayist Matthew Arnold, who
in *Culture and Anarchy* (1869) had defined these as the two
great spiritual disciplines of the West. Both, according to Arnold, aimed at "man's perfection or salvation," but in very
different ways. The Hellenic way was reason, seeing things "as
they really are"; the Hebraic way was behavior, "conduct and
obedience." Although Arnold appreciated Hebraism's virtues,
which he saw most fully realized in the Puritan ethic, his call
was for more Hellenism, for more high culture and disinter-
ested thought, which in his view Protestant civilization had
neglected since the Reformation. Niebuhr wanted just the opposite. Without denying the manifold contributions of Hellenism to modern life, he blamed it "for all our most serious
misunderstandings about man and his works." These were
chiefly two: the identification of the self with the mind, and
the belief that history proceeds on a rational pattern. Hebraism, with its personal God, its sense of covenant community,
and its memory of historical revelations, was far better
equipped to penetrate the mysteries of human existence. Hebraism showed man and his communities for the problematic
and imperfect entities they were; but while freeing humanity
from the illusions of perfectionism, it exalted the prophets'
refusal to abide the problems and the imperfections. This was
the essential contribution of "Hebraic-Christian culture," of
"Biblical-Christian awareness," of "Biblical Faith" to the
moral and political crises of the present age.[9]

The neo-orthodox emphasis on the Hebraic character of
Christianity played its part in fostering Judeo-Christian rheto-
ric during the war. At the early meetings of the Conference on
Science, Philosophy and Religion, for example, Nels Ferré,
John Bennett, and Amos Wilder all betrayed Niebuhrian influ-
ence in their invocations of Jewish-Christian faith. In due

course Paul Tillich, whose systematic theology relied on categories borrowed from classical metaphysics, would take Niebuhr to task for what he considered an overemphasis on Christianity's Hebraism. Tillich nevertheless endorsed Judeo-Christian ideology in Hebraist terms. "The Church," he wrote, was "always in danger of losing her prophetic spirit," and it therefore needed "the prophetic spirit included in the traditions of the synagogue . . . as long as the gods of space are in power, and this means up to the end of history." In "Is There a Judeo-Christian Tradition?," written in 1952 for the first issue of the journal *Judaism*, Tillich argued the affirmative by asserting that the two religions shared faith in an exclusive God, an understanding of man's historical existence, and the need to wrestle with "a legalistic and utopian interpretation of righteousness." [10]

Neo-orthodoxy insisted on the limited and historically conditioned character of all earthly institutions. The great sin, endemic to humanity, lay in treating the contingent as absolute; this was idolatry. The great virtue, embodied in the prophetic tradition, was constantly to question society's false absolutes in the name of the only true absolute, the God who transcended history. And among the false absolutes were the Church and its theology. Christianity as an institution embedded in history needed to be modest about its exclusive claims to truth—especially vis-à-vis Judaism. Tillich held that Christianity could be seen as a Jewish heresy and Judaism as a Christian one, and this position was adopted by Niebuhr as well: "At best, the two can regard themselves as two versions of one faith, each thinking of the other as an heretical version of the common faith." But if the other version of the common faith was heresy, of what use was it? In *Christianity and the Children of Israel* (1948), A. Roy Eckardt proposed a kind of division of labor, elaborating a neo-orthodox "theology for the Jewish question" that pointed to "the peculiar function which Judaism performs in the divine economy, that of testifying on behalf of a universal God of justice." Since Christianity characteristically attempted to limit grace to a particular historical reality, "We are confronted with the paradoxical fact that, while Christianity originally broke away from Judaism partly for the purpose of universalizing the Judaeo-Christian message, today Judaism has the function of protesting on behalf of universalism against the particularization of that message by Christianity." Judaism was essential if the Judeo-Christian message was to get across.[11]

Jewish writers did not fail to grasp the outstretched hand. During the war, the novelist and critic Waldo Frank allied himself with the neo-orthodox in calling for a convergence of Judaism and Christianity:

> I do not refer of course to the false convergences of Jews, "freed" of the Synagogue and of gentiles, "freed" of their churches, who meet upon the flat lands of empiricism. I do not refer to the pastors who shallow Jesus into a "very good man" or to the rabbis who assimilate Judaism to tepid Protestantism and ethical culture. I do refer to profound men of a new militant Church like Paul Tillich and Reinhold Niebuhr: religious minds who read the great stories of both Testaments as psychological truth beyond rationalist concepts; truth which reveals the insufficiency of empiric thought to explain the organic truth of man that only man's flesh and blood can utter.

Frank wanted his people to acquire a new appreciation of Jesus ("the finest personal flower of Jewish wisdom"), but he did not expect Jews to become Christians or vice versa. They should rather be "two harmonious minorities in an overwhelmed and menacing world." Though opposed to religious liberalism, Frank was not a traditionally observant Jew, and neither was Alfred Kazin, on whom the spirit of neo-orthodoxy alighted in *Partisan Review*'s 1950 symposium on "Religion and the Intellectuals." "Obviously, then," Kazin summed up his position, "I do believe in 'prophetic' rather than in 'institutional' religion; and, moreover, that the central and enduring values do stem from, even where they are no longer consciously tied to, the prophetic tradition of Judaism and Christianity."[12]

Yet it was not only to nonobservant Jewish intellectuals that the neo-orthodox outlook appealed. Abraham Heschel, professor at the Jewish Theological Seminary and the leading Conservative Jewish thinker of the time, took a Niebuhrian approach to the problem of sin in his major theological treatise, *God in Search of Man* (1955). Although he criticized the Christian theologian for underestimating the importance in "the Hebraic tradition" of the *mitzvah* (the divine commandment, the carrying out of a sacred deed) "as the instrument in dealing with evil," he nonetheless argued that Judaism shared Niebuhr's central conviction of the inescapable confusion of good and evil in human existence. When it came to Jewish proponents of neo-orthodox Hebraism, however, no one could surpass Will Herberg. Herberg had been a prominent Communist activist and theoretician, but in the late thirties his Marxist faith collapsed and he turned to religion—as a result, he claimed, of reading Niebuhr. He entertained the possibility of converting to Christianity but was dissuaded by Niebuhr himself, who told him he could not become a good Christian until he was first a good Jew. Returning to Judaism, Herberg began to write theology, and in 1955 was named Professor of Judaic Studies and Social Philosophy at (Methodist) Drew University.[13]

Judaism and Modern Man (1951) was Herberg's "confession of faith," and from its conception of the human predicament to its critique of Hellenism and secular liberalism, the confession went beyond the particular faith of Judaism. Herberg emphasized at the outset that while the terms "Jewish religion" and "Jewish faith" would be used for "the specific structure of Jewish spirituality," "Hebraic religion" and "biblical faith" were meant "to express the fundamental religious affirmation and commitment held in common by Judaism and Christianity." The following year he surveyed the extent of that common holding in an address before the American Academy of Religion entitled "Judaism and Christianity: Their Unity and Differences." Drawing largely on the ideas of the German-Jewish philosopher Franz Rosenzweig, Herberg concluded that the two faiths "represent one religious reality, Judaism facing inward to the Jews and Christianity facing outward to the gentiles, who, through it, are brought to the

God and under the covenant of Israel, and therefore cease to be gentiles." One religious reality did not mean one religion. The differences between a Christ-centered Christianity and a Judaism centered on God's covenant with Israel were real and irreducible, and must persist "until the final clarification." American society would evidently persist as the "triple melting pot" portrayed by Herberg in his widely read Protestant Catholic Jew (1955). Yet while setting a stamp of approval on the country's plural religious order, that book too ended with an impassioned avowal of "Jewish-Christian faith." In the final analysis, that was the real thing, the authentic faith needed "to transform the inner character of American religion."[14]

The seers of prophetic Hebraism were not cloistered academics discoursing privately with one another; they included celebrity theologians on the order of Jonathan Edwards in the eighteenth century and Horace Bushnell in the nineteenth. It was Niebuhr who graced the cover of Time magazine's twenty-fifth anniversary issue in 1948, and he and Tillich in particular were called upon to pronounce on any and all questions of faith and morals. In endowing "the Judeo-Christian tradition" with intellectual substance and intellectual respectability, the neo-orthodox theologians helped fashion the religious consensus that marks postwar American culture.

To be sure, their Judeo-Christian enterprise had its recusants. On the Jewish side, Robert Gordis, writing in 1955, could take up cudgels in behalf of "Hebraic-Christian heritage" and "the Judaeo-Christian tradition" by citing the common history of the two religions and "the debt that democracy owes to the Hebraic tradition"; but, in a swipe at Herberg, he denied that the Jewish principle of tschuvah—the turning from sin and return to God—required "a complete break with modernism, as we are exhorted in certain circles, and the enunciation of a 'post-modern' religious philosophy, which explains its affinities for Christian neo-Orthodoxy by constructing a cloudy, blurred image of an imaginary 'Judeo-Christian world view.'" Similarly, Alexander J. Burnstein argued that Niebuhr's central theological ideas could not be "consistently combined with the teachings of the Hebrew scriptures and normative Judaism." *Tschuvah*, which expressed man's "extraordinary capacity for good," was fundamentally at odds with the Niebuhrian stress on man's "frightening iniquity and spiritual impotence." The persistent concern of such writers was to prevent enthusiasm for the Judeo-Christian from blurring the distinctiveness of Judaism. Bernard Heller thus praised Paul Tillich for emphasizing the Church's need of "the prophetic spirit included in the tradition of the Synagogue," but attacked him for seeming to downplay the difference between Christian devotion to Christ and Jewish devotion to Torah. Judaism, asserted Heller, "refuses to accept the kiss of death."[15]

More powerful objections came from the Roman Catholics, whose *philosophia perennis* required no neo-orthodox infusion to save it from theological liberalism, or from anything else, for that matter. Indeed, "Hebraic faith" contained much that was repugnant. Its assault on Hellenic modes of thought (including natural law) extended to Thomism, which was nothing if not Hellenic; and prior to the Second Vatican Council, Thomism reigned supreme in Catholic theology. The neo-orthodox also took issue with the role assumed by the Roman hierarchy. In Niebuhr's words, "When an institution which mediates the judgment of God upon all the ambiguities of historic existence claims that it has escaped those ambiguities by this mission, it commits the same sin which the prophets recognized so clearly as the sin of Israel." The prime embodiment of that sin was, of course, the papacy. Ever since the Pope had claimed to be Christ's vicar on earth, "Christianity has been inferior to Hebraic prophetism in failing to observe a proper distance between the divine and the human." Under the circumstances, even John Courtney Murray, Catholicism's lonely champion of religious pluralism in the 1950s, could have no use for the Jewish-Christian faith of Niebuhr and company. In *We Hold These Truths*, a collection of essays that adds up to a defense of natural law against its neo-orthodox critics, Murray held that Protestantism, Catholicism, and Judaism were "radically different" styles of religious belief, none of which "is reducible, or perhaps even comparable, to any of the others." The best that might be hoped for was "creeds at war intelligibly" under "the articles of peace which are the religion-clauses of the First Amendment."[16]

Roman Catholic invocation of "the Judeo-Christian tradition" often amounted to no more than an acknowledgment of the Jewish roots of Christianity. Typical was Jacques Maritain's assertion, in Partisan Review's "religion and the intellectuals" symposium, that people "are becoming aware of the fact that no real radical movement in politics and no fundamental social improvements are to be brought about without the spiritual energies and the basic humanist tenets inseparable from the Judeo-Christian religious tradition, and that democracy can only live on Christianity." The energies and the tenets might derive from Judaism, but the sustaining reality was Christian.[17]

This sort of Judeo-Christian Catholicism found its preeminent expression in the Institute of Judaeo-Christian Studies, which was established in 1953 at Seton Hall University in New Jersey under the direction of the Jewish convert and priest John M. Oesterreicher. Oesterreicher was a longtime promoter of Catholic—Jewish understanding, a liberal who enthusiastically applauded Pope John XXIII's removal of the adjective perfidis from the Good Friday prayer for "the perfidious [that is, unbelieving] Jews." The Institute's yearbook, The Bridge, featured articles on Jewish subjects by Catholic authors, designed to enhance Christian appreciation of Jewish culture and to stimulate discussion between Christians and Jews. Nevertheless, the final purpose of the Institute was, said Oesterreicher, "to bring our age back to Christ." It sought, according to the Jesuit weekly America, "not to remove the stumblingblock of the cross, but to reveal it as the very bridge over which Israel must pass in order to enter into the promise." While eschewing overt proselytization, the Judaeo-Christian Institute was dedicated "to an intellectual apostolate calculated to facilitate the passage of the old to the new." As far a cry as this was from neo-orthodox Hebraism, it yet underlined the power of the formula. As with other religious formulas, its meaning could be debated—or it could be merely uttered as a shibboleth; like it or not, the Judeo-Christian tradition had become the true emblem of America's adhesional faith.[18]

But what was there besides adhesional faith in the chilly dawn of "tomorrow's better world"? As postwar America made for the suburbs, did the settlers need all those churches no less, but no more, than they needed country clubs and Little League, to fashion themselves into communities? Did the American family, worshiping in the church of its choice, pray together only—or even—to stay together? "I looked around me, and wondered what their religion really meant to the commuters I saw on every hand," wrote the novelist Peter DeVries, describing a church supper on the new suburban frontier. "I have never heard of anything being converted in Connecticut except old barns."[19] Yet the Fourth Great Awakening did not lack for strong messages of conversion. Faced with the powerful adhesional pressures, some proved widely appealing; and others were intolerable.

3 ∎ THE WAGES OF CONVERSION (I)

O N Sunday afternoon, September 25, 1949, in a huge tent newly erected on a vacant lot at the edge of town, a flamboyant thirty-one-year-old preacher stood up to inaugurate the latest in a series of revivals he had been conducting around the country. His subject was "The Choice That Is Before Los Angeles During These Next Three Weeks," and for twenty-one days the city of the angels gave a satisfactory enough account of itself. The "canvas cathedral," capable of holding six thousand souls, averaged two-thirds capacity, and fifteen hundred people hit the sawdust trail to accept Jesus Christ as their personal lord and savior. For all the advertising on radio and in the newspapers, however, the event was not big news; the papers limited themselves to a few back-page articles on what seemed of interest only to the local evangelical community— just the latest exhibit in Southern California's varied religious menagerie. Then, shortly after the sponsoring organization (the Christ for Greater Los Angeles Committee) announced a "Fourth Great Week by Popular Demand," the evangelist arrived for his nightly performance to find the tent teeming with reporters and photographers. "You've been kissed," he was told, "by William Randolph Hearst." Exiled on doctor's orders from his beloved San Simeon to a house in Beverly Hills, the eighty-six-year-old press lord, diseased of heart but firm of mind, had dispatched his minions with a two-word memo: "Puff Graham."

Thanks to banner headlines in the *Examiner* and *Herald-Express*, and aided by the conversion of a few local celebrities, the Reverend William Franklin Graham, Jr., became the hottest show in town, held over, now by real popular demand, for eight weeks. And from the Hearst papers the word went forth: to *Time* and *Life*, to *Newsweek* and *Quick*, to everyone carrying the Associated Press wire. For the first time in decades— since Billy Sunday, the acrobatic former major-league baseball player, had peaked during World War I—an evangelist was national news. Billy Graham had become William Randolph Hearst's last gift to the American people.

Why should Hearst, a nominal Episcopalian of no particular religious enthusiasm, have chosen to promote an evangelist? And why this particular one?

Four years earlier, Graham had emerged as one of the leaders of Youth for Christ, a new evangelical movement whose weekly Saturday-night rallies featured, along with the message of Jesus, lively musical entertainment and plenty of patriotic flag-waving. Its fundamentalist organizers saw it as a way of turning teenaged America from the evils of alcohol, tobacco, the jitterbug, and juvenile delinquency back to the old-time religion. Whatever he thought of Jesus, Hearst loved to promote conventional morality and fervid Americanism, and his papers had enthusiastically promoted Youth for Christ; in 1946, when Graham made the first of six trips to bring the YFC gospel to war-torn Europe, a Hearst reporter accompanied the entourage. By 1947, there were semiautonomous YFC organizations in a thousand American cities. Graham, who had blanketed the country as the movement's first "official field representative," now struck out on his own as a conductor of the more traditional kind of revival. So he was not unknown to Hearst when he turned up in L.A.

From Los Angeles, Graham proceeded to Boston, where

the Reverend Harold Ockenga, one of his mentors, presided over the Park Street Church. There he received vast press coverage and filled hall after successively larger hall to overflowing; on January 16, sixteen thousand people squeezed into Boston Garden to hear the new religious phenomenon, and thousands more were turned away. Then it was on to Columbia, South Carolina, where Dixiecrat Governor Strom Thurmond endorsed the crusade, made the young preacher his houseguest, and brought prominent Carolinians into the tent. On March 1, Graham issued his call for revival to a joint session of the state legislature. Down at his baronial retreat on the coast, so the story goes, the aging Jewish financier Bernard Baruch read Graham's address in the newspaper and called it to the attention of Henry Luce, then vacationing with Clare— an old flame of Baruch's—at the Yeaman's Hall Club near Charleston. Where Baruch was ambivalent about religion and mistrustful of prayerful men in public life, Luce was always on the lookout for anything that might betoken a revival of religion in America.[1] Summoning William Howland, his Atlanta bureau chief, he quickly arranged to drive up to Columbia. On March 9, after dining with the Thurmonds and attending the evening session of the crusade, Luce kept Graham up late talking theology. As Graham's longtime associate Grady Wilson recalled, he "watched Billy like a hawk."

Years later, Graham described his encounter with Luce as lasting several days. "We stayed up each night until one or two in the morning, talking alone, for two or three nights. I think he was trying to pull me out to see if I was genuine or honest. At that time, frankly, I didn't really know who he was. But boy, did I respect him." However long the examination took— Howland remembered only a one-night stand—Graham passed with flying colors. Though *Time* had run an item on the Los Angeles crusade, it was something else to enjoy the personal favor of the boss. On his return to Charleston, Luce ordered up stories for both his famous weeklies. "*Time* and *Life*," said Graham, "they began carrying about everything I did, it seemed like. They gave me a tremendous push." In the years to come, whenever he happened to be in New York,

Graham would drop in on Luce. "I think he took a sort of fatherly interest in me almost. When he appointed Hedley Donovan to begin running everything, he called me up there and took me in and introduced me to Donovan and said, 'Now, when there's anything you want, you come to him just as you would to me.' "[2]

Graham had impressed Luce, as he would impress all who tried to take his measure, as the genuine article. Here was a man of faith, a tall blond evangelical Galahad whose earnest speech and clear-eyed gaze banished all thoughts of hypocrisy. He was modest, too, this North Carolina farm boy, conveying a kind of naive wonder at his sudden celebrity. To the Luce-man who covered him in South Carolina he gladly told the tale of the kiss of Hearst, as, later, he would tell a reporter for the *Charlotte Observer* of his vetting by Baruch and Luce.[3] Yet for all the public scrutiny, many continued to find Graham puzzling. Rural insouciant he might be, but his operation was slick and professional. He was an impassioned orator, but the vast crowds that came to hear him were calm and well behaved. And though a biblical literalist who preached The Fundamentals, he sought, and obtained, the support of mainline Protestants.

There was, in fact, nothing anomalous about any of it. As has been pointed out by William McLoughlin, the most historically informed of his biographers, Graham was walking a well-trodden path; his methods, his talent for publicity and for the support of the rich and powerful, his style, his doctrine, his (as it were) ecumenism—all were built on a century of evangelistic practice in the mainstream of American Protestantism. Since Scopes had blackened the name of fundamentalism, the mass revival had been out of fashion, even in the cities of the Bible Belt; and it survived, to the extent it did, as part of an apparently obsolescent subculture. "We are tired of religious revivals as we have known them in the last half century," wrote Dean Willard L. Sperry of the Harvard Divinity School in 1946. "Among all but the most backward churches it is now agreed that education ought to be, and probably is, the best way of interesting our people in religion and of identifying them with one or another of our many denominations."[4] Yet if the people themselves proved susceptible to Billy Graham, it was not only because they were out of step with the advanced thinking of the churches. Within just a few years the young revivalist had succeeded in breaching the strongest citadels of the Protestant establishment. That, to be sure, took some doing, and not least because he was closely associated with the National Association of Evangelicals for United Action, the organizational arm of what came to be known in the 1950s as the New Evangelicalism.

When the association was founded in 1943, *The Christian Century* had greeted it with the headline "Sectarianism Receives New Lease on Life." The leaders of the new body claimed that the great majority of those for whom the Federal Council of Churches "has presumed to speak" were misrepresented by the policies of that body. Nonsense, snapped the nondenominational weekly: "Every kind of conservatism" within the NAE could be found in bodies belonging to the FCC —"and this not in suppressed minorities or in inarticulate and misrepresented majorities, as the 'evangelicals' say, but in the personnel of every part of the organizational structure from top to bottom." As the *Century* saw it, the NAE's founders clearly desired not representation within a united Protestantism, but control of part of Protestantism's divided house.[5] During and just after the war, the chief preoccupation of the Protestant high command was institutionalizing ecumenism, what with the Federal Council of Churches about to grow into the National Council, and the World Council aborning. Efforts on the part of disaffected conservatives to organize in opposition could hardly fail to raise establishment hackles.

The NAE was not the only such effort. The American Council of Christian Churches had been set up one year earlier by a preacher from Collingswood, New Jersey, named Carl McIntire. Back in 1929, McIntire had followed his teacher, the fundamentalist divine J. Gresham Machen, when the latter decamped from Princeton Theological Seminary to restore Presbyterianism to its ancient strictness at Westminster Seminary in Chestnut Hill, Pennsylvania. In McIntire, however, a native strain of antiestablishmentarianism ran so pure that within a few years he broke with Machen and founded his own denomination. The American Council too manifested his radically oppositional character, becoming a kind of ecclesiastical *Doppelgänger* to the establishment's ecumenical bodies; whithersoever they assembled, there would the ACCC go, compelling the FCC or NCC or WCC to issue warnings to press and public not to labor under any confusion about which was which and what was what. Living to vituperate and harass, McIntire and his followers quintessentially embodied the paranoid style in American politics.

But if the ACCC represented the parodic termination of the fundamentalist–modernist battles of the twenties and early thirties, the NAE was the expression of the next generation. Its leaders, anxious to efface the stigma of fundamentalism (they shunned the term), were nonetheless confident that they had the right stuff for what ailed America. There was, however, a stumbling block. As Carl Henry, the New Evangelicalism's leading theologian, put it in his 1947 tract *The Uneasy Conscience of Modern Fundamentalism,* "The force of the redemptive message will not break with apostolic power upon the modern scene unless the American Council of Churches and the National Association of Evangelicals meet at some modern Antioch, and Peter and Paul are face to face in a spirit of mutual love and compassion. If, as is often remarked, the Federal Council of Churches is the voice of Protestant liberalism in America, Protestant evangelicalism too needs a single voice."

Was this more than pious rhetoric? Given the temperament of Carl McIntire, one might have concluded that an amalgamation of NAE and ACCC was as undesirable as it was impossible—that the NAE was better off challenging the establishment on its own. And so, perforce, it did. In 1948, committees of both the Reformed Church in America and the United Presbyterian Church (not to be confused with the 1958 Presbyterian amalgamation of the same name) met to study the relative merits of remaining in the Federal Council and switching to the NAE. The same year, the question of membership in the FCC was put before the presbyteries of the Presbyterian Church in the United States. Yet none of the three chose to run up different interdenominational colors, and it was soon plain that the NAE was not about to give mainline ecumenism a head-to-head run for its money.[6] There were, however, other ways of doing battle.

Day in and day out, editor James DeForest Murch of *United Evangelical Action*, the official NAE organ, anathematized the National Council of Churches as an ominous "superchurch." Significantly, though, the NAE did not seek to burn all bridges to the establishment in the manner of the ACCC. "The latter," noted *The Christian Century*, "insists that its members must not only repudiate and denounce apostasy (i.e., the National Council), but also separate from it. The NAE settles for repudiation and denunciation." If it could not enlist entire denominations, the NAE was prepared to sign up individuals, schools, missions, and congregations whose parent bodies belonged to the National Council; it was, in effect, bent on raiding behind NCC lines—and notably in the matter of fund-raising. In the mid-1950s, the Reverend J. Kenneth Miller, a Long Island minister who served on the United Presbyterian Church's World Service Committee, forwarded a couple of dunning letters he had received from NAE organizations to H. J. McKnight, a fellow committee member (and UP representative to the National Council's Joint Department of Stewardship and Benevolence). Miller complained of the NAE's ethics in trying to siphon funds from a denomination possessed of its own competing benevolent and interchurch institutions, but ecclesiological punctilio was not his only concern. "This N.A.E. outfit," he wrote of the World Evangelical Fellowship in 1956, "has influence in this Synod."[7]

It was, thus, as the cynosure of forces maneuvering against mainline ecumenism that Billy Graham was first viewed by establishmentarians. *The Christian Century* took note of his presence at the NAE conventions of 1951, 1952, and 1953. An article on the effects of his 1951 Seattle crusade was warily noncommittal. The enthusiasm that greeted Graham at the 1952 Southern Baptist Convention in San Francisco left the journal cold—especially when "the most popular young evangelist of the day . . . mopped his brow and cried, 'When this convention voted earlier this week not to affiliate with any other group, I thanked God.' " The vote in question was to ratify a committee report which, among other things, attacked both the National and the World councils; it was, said the Century's correspondent, "the most perverse, unbrotherly and dangerous pronouncement made by any Southern Baptist Convention in many years." But then, on March 24, 1954, with Graham playing to overflow houses across the Atlantic, came the following: "In London as in America, Billy Graham is revealing himself as extraordinarily teachable and humble, considering that he is surrounded with the fevered adulation of crowds so much of the time. He will learn a great deal in London, and will, if he keeps up the growth which has characterized his last three years, put what he learns to good use for Christ and the church." How to explain the change of heart?[8]

Just one month earlier Graham had ventured into the theological lion's den—New York's Union Theological Seminary—and after speaking in chapel for forty-five minutes and answering questions in the Social Room for another thirty, had come away with one of the greatest ovations in recent memory. Had news of the encounter reached the Century's editors in Chicago? Whatever, their new image of the "educable" Graham mirrored what John Bennett had to say in "Billy Graham at Union," in the May number of the Union Seminary Quarterly Review. To explain the applause, Union's dean of faculty pointed to Graham's manifest sincerity and magnetism, his verbal adroitness, and the simple relief of his audience at finding him not as bad as they feared. Yet underneath it all, said Bennett, there was reason to think that Graham was "breaking the pattern" of the crude and mercenary evangelist: "many of us gained the strong impression that he can be used for highly constructive Christian purposes in the churches and in the nation."

For Bennett, "breaking the pattern" meant that Graham understood the limits of mass evangelism and the importance of honest financial management. It also meant—at least, he hoped it did—that Graham's grasp of "biblical truth" would be sufficient to correct his enthusiasm for America's "culture religion" (exemplified in his laugh-provoking claim that the American Legion's Back-to-God Campaign signaled a national religious awakening); and that his "ecumenical outlook and strategy" (the word "ecumenical" recurred often in his remarks) might "deliver him from the worst effects of Fundamentalism." In any case, Graham's use of the Bible did not represent a "hard Fundamentalism," and there was evidence that he was "growing" in his social outlook. "I am publishing this article with some hesitation," Bennett concluded.

> I do not like to set myself up as a judge of Billy Graham in this way and I do not want this record of my surprise to seem patronizing. It is a fact that until his visit to Union I had classed him as a fundamentalist and socially reactionary evangelist and had dismissed him as a possible constructive force in the American Church. On the other hand there is a chance that this article may be too optimistic and hence misleading. . . . When all is said, I believe that his coming to Union was a very good lesson for us. It may have helped us to realize more vividly, what we should have known from Church History, that God can work powerfully through men who do not meet all our specifications.

The New Evangelicalism's Galahad had won a provisional seat at the establishment's Round Table.[9]

The consequences could be discerned in the great ecumenical bodies. In August of the same year, at the Second Assembly of the World Council of Churches in Evanston, no phase of the program received more attention than the report of Section II, "The Mission of the Church to Those Outside Her Life"; extra time was allotted for comment on the delicate question of how to set policy for trans-church evangelism.[10] In the spring, meanwhile, the National Council had appointed Berlyn Farris, an old-fashioned evangelical Methodist from Wichita, to be executive director of its Department of Evangelism. Having declared, in May, that "today's climate for the evangelistic work of the churches is the most favorable we've had in America in the last 20 years," Farris spelled out, in a year-end report, just what he had in mind for the nation's cities.

>   Let us dream a moment. Suppose in a given city a National Christian Teaching Mission would first go in to make a gigantic survey, establish the mood of evangelism in every church in the city and prepare the way for a great movement of evangelism. Following that would be an organized prayer program which would be extended into every block of the entire city. A Visitation Evangelism program would come in, following the spiritual development which would undoubtedly bring hundreds of persons into the acceptance of Jesus Christ and the fellowship of the Church. This would be followed by a great program of preaching with an evangelist who could proclaim nightly the saving power of Jesus Christ.
>   This would be a revival in the truest sense of the word, not only winning persons to the acceptance of Christ for the first time, but a deepening of the spiritual life of the multitudes of the city. This would then be followed by a program of stewardship, encouraging the people to tithe, to attend church, to pray, and to serve. Thus the whole community would be awakened and the Church and Christian life of the community would be deepened. This is a dream, to be sure. But isn't it the sort of stuff that reality is made of?

Such rhetoric had not been heard from Protestant headquarters in New York for many years.[11]

A case can be made that during the mid-fifties a kind of conversionist excitement took hold in mainline Protestantism which harked back to the days before Scopes, when "the evangelization of the world in this generation" was a goal that establishmentarians could happily embrace. With liberalism (read: modernism) on the run in the loftiest theological circles, those who professed The Fundamentals were no longer so easily dismissed; by his classic revivalist's willingness to ignore doctrinal and institutional barriers in gathering his forces, Graham proved capable of enlisting the support not only of layfolk but also of sophisticated clergy across the denominations of the NCC. It was also the hour of the American Century (as proclaimed by Henry Luce, the China missionary's son), when the country was eager to think of itself as leading a struggle against dark, atheistic powers at loose in the world. Why not a return to the yoked advance of American power and American religion, with Billy Graham as minister-in-chief?

In part, Graham owed his popularity to deft spiritual politics. He had a knack for moving lightly between his evangelical and his ecumenical friends, speaking to each in the language they liked to hear. Though criticized from both the antievangelical left and the uncompromising fundamentalist right, he always turned the other cheek; and internecine religious conflict found him strictly aloof. With the exception of the race issue, where he was a bit of a liberal, his secular politics were generally those of any conservative Southern Democrat of the time; but his sermons, while filled with topical commentary, stopped short of partisan controversy. Despite temptation, he never allowed himself to make an explicit political endorsement. Concerned as he was with the morals of his compatriots, he understood the importance of keeping himself, like Caesar's wife, above suspicion; the suspicion of profiteering, downfall of many an earlier evangelist, he avoided by forswearing solicitation of "freewill offerings" and arranging instead to be paid a fixed annual salary. And his employer, the Billy Graham Evangelistic Association, was itself a model of propriety.

But to understand Graham's remarkable success it is necessary to look beyond his good luck with the press, personal charisma, tried and true evangelistic techniques, and determination to keep his own house in order—to what he actually said. For his was a call for conversion pitched perfectly to the adhesional needs of the moment. Here, for example, is how he preached in Los Angeles that September 25, 1949, two days after President Truman announced to the country that the Soviet Union had exploded its first atomic bomb.

America, he began, had escaped the ravages of war "because God's people," a people who believed that God could "still use America to evangelize the world," prayed. Now God was "giving us a desperate choice, a choice of either revival or judgment." The "entire world" had been shocked by news of the Soviet bomb.

> An arms race, unprecedented in the history of the world, is driving us madly toward destruction! And I sincerely believe that it is the providence of God that He has chosen this hour for a campaign—giving this city one more chance to repent of sin and turn to a believing knowledge of the Lord Jesus Christ.

Once our country had claimed the Ten Commandments as the basis of its moral code; now divorce, crime, sex, gambling, drinking, and juvenile delinquency were rampant. The world was "divided into two sides": Western culture, founded in religion, and Communism, against all religion. On a visit to Parliament three months earlier "a British statesman" had told him of his government's conviction that our civilization would be ended in five to ten years. (And that "was before he heard that Russia has the atomic bomb.") Los Angeles was filled with false prophets and false cults, filled with citizens who said they believed in God but did not go to church. God had destroyed Sodom and Gomorrah, and Pompeii too. His wrath, in the form of an earthquake or a tidal wave, might likewise descend upon the city; it also happened to be third (after New York and Chicago) on the enemy's slate for atomic destruction. But repentance could still avert the evil decree, as it had been averted in Nineveh or, for that matter, in England itself, where the preaching of John Wesley and George Whitefield had precipitated a revival sufficient to stave off the evils of the French Revolution.

Revival would take place if people recognized the need, repented of their sins, prayed, and had faith. The result would be a new missionary emphasis in the church, new church members, Christian unity, and "tremendous social implications." Did you know, asked Graham, that the abolition of slavery and child labor, a shorter work week, trade unions, the YMCA and Salvation Army, most charitable institutions and many educational ones, slum-clearance programs, the Sunday School, and women's suffrage were all "revival results"? Nothing was required but to turn to Jesus. "Let Christ come into your heart and cleanse you from sin, and He can give you the assurance that if you died tonight, you would go to heaven. We call this belief in Christ salvation—*anyone* can be saved by simply believing that the Lord Jesus Christ suffered and died for his sin."[12]

Preached prior to all the national attention, the sermon shows Graham's distinctive homiletic style already formed. What he did was attach the revivalist's traditional call for individual repentance to a circumstantial account of collective decay and doom. It was, in fact, a rhetorical mode that went back to the very origins of the culture. From the time the Puritans first set foot in New England, they found themselves subjected to what were, in effect, "state of the covenant" addresses. Through a litany of moral turpitude and woeful current events the preachers would go, indicating, in the manner of the prophet Jeremiah, just how far the community was failing to fulfill its sacred errand into the wilderness. Yet these jeremiads, as they were called, were not despairing; in the very act of specifying the lapses, they reasserted and reaffirmed the errand. And, as modern scholars have recognized, they left a permanent mark on American culture. Long after the Puritans and their Calvinist theology were gone, there remained the habit of inveighing against the sins of the nation in a way that emphasized the special character, the transcendent mission, the dream, of America.[13] Indeed, if the heart of the Judeo-Christian tradition was Hebraic prophetism, nowhere was it more deeply embedded in the culture than in the form of the American jeremiad.

Of Graham's great nineteenth- and twentieth-century predecessors, none—not Billy Sunday, Dwight L. Moody, or Charles G. Finney himself—employed in his revival sermons the sort of premonitory evidence of national disaster that Graham did. Their focus throughout had been on the conversion of the particular sinner, and from them Graham inherited the conviction, known in Protestant theology as Arminianism, that the individual cooperates in the work of his own redemption. You had only to believe, you had only to turn to Jesus, and you would be saved. Incorporating this news into his wide-ranging jeremiads, Graham put much more in the hands of his listeners: a mass of public benefits and the staying of God's wrath against all humankind. It was not merely that revival, as a collective phenomenon, could be expected to have collective results. "You say, 'But Billy, I'm only one person.' Ah, yes, but when you make your decision, it is America through you making its decision."[14] America, avatar of individualism, expressed itself through the individual, and one American's conversion bespoke a national will to reform.

This was, as the American jeremiad had always been, an ultimately upbeat message. For all the depravity and bleakness, the promise remained intact, and actually within our grasp. In "Whither bound?," a sermon given on January 31, 1950, Graham began by rehearsing what made the present hour the most foreboding in the nation's history: the threat of being invaded and bombed, a disastrous war in Korea, the prospect of a lower standard of living, moral deterioration, a lethargic Church. Yet the new year offered, he said, three "possibilities," which he went on to describe as "alternatives." The first was further war and deterioration; the second, spiritual revival; and the third, the Second Coming. Graham did not claim that Americans could actually select the last of these; God alone appointed and knew the time. But alternative meant choice, and the implication was that in some obscure way Americans might, even here, help choose.[15]

One of Graham's early promotional books contains a photograph of the evangelist behind a pulpit in an airplane aisle, dedicating Chicago and Southern Airlines' brand-new Constellation high above Memphis. What business was this of his? Could the conversion he preached mean much if Jeremiah was on such cozy terms with the culture he denounced? "I could tell you of a movie star in Hollywood, or the congressman in Washington, or the state senator from Georgia, or the all-American basketball star from Washington. I could tell you about the multi-millionaire in New England, the brilliant Harvard and Yale students who have made their way down the long aisles saying 'yes' to Christ." Graham loved to cite (without naming names) the wealthy and the famous and the talented who had made their conversions. That, to him, was an enrichment, not a rejection, of their previous lives. To dedicate an airplane was to sanctify it and the American way of life that made it possible. Invited to pray in Congress in April of 1950, Graham thanked God for "this greatest nation in the world."[16]

Early in 1952 Graham met Dwight D. Eisenhower, urged him to run for president, gave him a Bible, and became something of an adviser. During the election campaign, Ike asked for his advice about which denomination to join, saying that he did not believe the American people would follow a president who was not a member of a church. Graham suggested that he become a Presbyterian, which he did. After the election, the evangelist told his "Hour of Decison" radio audience how deeply impressed he was with the president-elect's sincerity, humility, and grasp of world affairs. "I also sensed a dependence upon God. He told me on both occasions that the hope of building a better America lay in a spiritual revival." Inaugurated on a Sunday, Eisenhower concluded his address with a prayer; Graham, on the radio, declared that as a result the American people felt "a little more secure, realizing we have a man who believes in prayer at the helm of our government at this crucial hour."[17]

Though his sermons would continue to paint pictures of impending doom, Graham's effective message, in word and deed, was the positive side of the jeremiad—the side that said, yes, everything could be all right; the country's destiny could still be; the government, indeed, was in good hands; all that was needed now was your individual cooperation. As a regular at White House receptions and presidential rounds of golf, the evangelist represented an assurance of available spiritual resources: the prophet assumed a priestly role. For many Protestants he became, in William McLoughlin's words, "the same kind of symbol of faith and hope in the chaotic world that Pope Pius XII was for Roman Catholics."[18] Conversion à la Billy became its own ritual of adhesion; to accept Billy's Christ was to keep faith with those of other denominations, with the government, with America itself. Judeo-Christian in the full ecumenical sense it may not have been, but in the postwar situation this was the kind of conversionist message that could prosper.

4 ■ THE WAGES OF CONVERSION (II)

O N Monday evening, April 5, 1948, Richard J. Cushing, the archbishop of Boston, came to dine at Lowell House, one of the undergraduate residences of Harvard College. The occasion was High Table, a weekly ritual instituted two decades before by Lowell's first master, mathematics professor Julian Lowell Coolidge. Concerned that a Harvard house be more than a mere college dormitory, and inspired by the example of Balliol College, Oxford, where he had done graduate work, Coolidge used High Table to exhibit faculty and distinguished guests to the young men in his charge. Nor was Cushing the first occupant of the see of Boston to grace the Lowell House dining hall. William Cardinal O'Connell himself had put in an appearance, for Coolidge, though the stiffest of Unitarian bluebloods, had been (through his aunt, the art-collecting Mrs. Gardner) a good friend of that lordly prince of the Church.[1] Nevertheless, when Coolidge's successor in the mastership, Elliott Perkins, extended an invitation to O'Connell's successor, both knew that more was at stake than the continuation of a small tradition of goodwill between university and archdiocese. Since the end of the war, Harvard's peace of mind had been increasingly disturbed by the activities on its doorstep of the Catholic organization called St. Benedict Center. Now the Boston hierarchy was becoming disturbed as well.

St. Benedict Center had sprung into existence innocuously enough. In 1940, a devout laywoman named Catherine Clarke, together with a couple of Harvard students, had secured local ecclesiastical permission to set up a gathering place for Catholic collegians in a vacant furniture shop one block from Harvard Yard and across the street from the parish church, St. Paul's. Before long, a lively social and intellectual life was under way. Informal courses were organized in theology, philosophy, and Church Latin. Mrs. Clarke gave afternoon teas. One of the founding members was Avery Dulles, John Foster's son, who after a brilliant college career was in the process of converting to Roman Catholicism. Dulles had proposed that the center be named after the Jesuit saint Robert Bellarmine, but this Counter-Reformation controversialist was deemed too offensive to Protestant sensibilities, and the more neutral monastic figure of Saint Benedict was selected instead.

After Pearl Harbor, Dulles and many other regulars went off to war, but under Mrs. Clarke's steadfast hand the center prospered. Students from throughout the Boston area came to attend talks and seminars offered by interested Catholic faculty from Harvard. Celebrities like Dorothy Day and Mrs. Luce were invited to speak. And among these early visitors to the center was a bantam-sized Jesuit named Leonard Feeney. Feeney was a minor celebrity. His verse, singsong and inspirational, was a staple of Catholic primary and secondary schools, and *Fish on Fridays*, a collection of sketches and stories on Catholic themes, had been a national best-seller in 1934. During the late thirties, Feeney was the literary editor of *America*, from which post he carried on a campaign against modern culture after the manner of his literary idol, G. K. Chesterton. Chosen president of the Catholic Poetry Society in 1940, he was transferred to the faculty of the Jesuit college in Weston, Massachusetts, where his superiors expected him to put some life into the homiletics curriculum. There was another reason for sending the poetical priest back to his native Massachusetts as well. He could not hold his liquor, and the intention was for him to dry out.

Although it was the jewel in the crown of American Jesuit education, Weston did not thrill Feeney, nor could the college lecture circuit and radio appearances on "The Catholic Hour" compensate for the life of a literary lion in New York. On the wagon and thirsty for excitement, he latched on to St. Benedict Center, attending courses, volunteering pastoral counseling, and in due course making himself an indispensable source of doctrinal instruction and authority. In 1945, after a friend obtained a blessing on the center from the Pope, Mrs. Clarke screwed up her courage to ask that Father Feeney be assigned to St. Benedict's full time. Thanks to the support of Monsignor John J. Wright, a rising archdiocesan official and frequent visitor to the center, she got her way.

When Avery Dulles returned from the Navy in 1946, he found the place teeming with activity. The main event was Feeney's Thursday-night lecture, a command performance that week after week held hundreds spellbound for two to three hours. "Never have I known a speaker with such a sense of collective psychology," Dulles later wrote. "In the early part of his lectures he would tell anecdotes, recite poems and in various ways seek to gain the attention and good will of all his hearers." (A talented mimic, Feeney convulsed his audience with impressions of famous people in improbable situations: Katharine Hepburn reporting a prizefight, FDR lamenting the decline of sacramental religion, Fulton Sheen declaiming the merits of Coca-Cola—"Ho, everyone that thirsteth for the pause that refresheth!") "Totally aware of the reactions of every person in the room, he would focus his attention especially on those who seemed hostile, indifferent or distracted. When at length he had the entire audience reacting as a unit, he would launch into the main body of his talk, leading them from insight to insight, from emotion to emotion, until all were carried away, as if by an invisible force permeating the atmosphere."[2] When it came to his close disciples, Feeney acted, according to Dulles, like an old-fashioned Jesuit novice master, directing every aspect of their personal and intellectual development. But in public or in private his teaching was the same: systematic, unambiguous, and harsh toward anything that smacked of liberalism. He also had a particular thing about Jews.

"After the war," recalled one of the disciples, "everything was chaos, and all the boys were returning to college. But the secular teachings were equally confusing. . . ." [3] Since well before the war, academic reformers like Robert Hutchins and Alexander Meiklejohn had been assailing the intellectual disarray of American college education, and in 1946 Harvard itself inaugurated a general-education program which, in a windy and widely publicized report, called for coherent instruction in the Western tradition. Religion, however, was not on the pedagogical agenda of the school that three generations earlier had led American higher education in abolishing compulsory chapel. (The Bible could not secure a place in its general-education curriculum even as great literature.) So St. Benedict Center had it all over Harvard when it came to the ultimate questions. Conversions to Roman Catholicism began to be made; in time there would be some two hundred. Center members began heading for religious orders and the priesthood; about a hundred would eventually do so. (Dulles himself joined the Jesuits in the summer of 1946, ultimately to become one of their leading American theologians.) Archbishop Cushing, who had for many years headed the Boston office of the Society for the Propagation of the Faith, could hardly fail to be delighted. He had known Feeney since student days together at Boston College High School. In the fall of 1946 he contributed two articles of his own to the center's new magazine, From the Housetops; in October of the following year he favored St. Benedict Center with a personal visit, and anointed Feeney's head with praise.

At the center, as in the Billy Graham crusades, the spirituality drew on national anxieties. "We were never quite the same . . . after the dropping of the atom bomb," wrote Catherine Clarke. "It seemed to have shocked us awake." The night the destruction of Hiroshima was announced, the center issued a statement of grief and condemnation. But where Graham portrayed the threat of atomic destruction as God's impending punishment for the collective sins of the world and of His chosen American people, St. Benedict's Roman Catholics saw it as the product of an evil alien to themselves. Again, Mrs. Clarke: "We waited and we listened, but no strong voice arose above the noise of the world. There was only the jubilant announcement of a new age, the atomic age, born out of the abandonment of a Christian principle!" And where Graham was happy to cite Harvard and Yale as sources of brilliant new conversions to Christ, for Feeney Harvard was cause and symbol of the evil times. The bomb, he would say, was simply the consequence of the secularism that Harvard taught. He liked to claim that Harvard President James Bryant Conant, a prominent figure in the Manhattan Project, had told a dinner party that "to make a more interesting experiment" the U.S. should have dropped ten atomic bombs on Japan. "There'll be," said Feeney, "a Third World War and another one after that because of these 'skeptical chemists' like Conant."[4]

Dulles, who had already written about his spiritual odyssey from Harvard liberalism to Roman Catholicism in a book entitled *A Testimonial to Grace*, set forth the center's outlook in the first issue of *From the Housetops*. "Every culture which is not Catholic is in some degree anti-Catholic. . . . Due to the infiltration of falsehood into the lower levels of our consciousness, our view of the universe tends to become half Christian and half miscreant. . . . The belief that one can with impunity consort constantly with heretics and atheists, and casually exchange ideas with them, is a dangerous product of modern liberalism." Another contributor was even blunter: "Our secular colleges are the expression and source of much that in our day strives to undermine the faith, life, and cultural heritage of Catholics." Such attitudes were hardly novel within American Catholicism, but some undergraduates, converts as well as born Catholics, were sufficiently fired up by Feeney to act on them; they resigned from Harvard and transferred to Catholic colleges in the area. Before long, however, the transfers began reporting back that their new schools were sick with the very infection from which they had fled. So St. Benedict Center became a degree-granting institution of learning in its own right, obtaining accreditation under the G.I. Bill to accommodate the many veterans in its membership. Feeney was now in a position to ensure that his followers imbibed only his own pure version of integral Catholic culture.[5]

Although by the standards of the late forties Catholic higher education in Boston could scarcely be considered liberal, Feeney had by 1947 decided that orthodoxy demanded an absolutist interpretation of the doctrine that there was no salvation outside the Church—*extra ecclesiam nulla salus.* This doctrine, first articulated in the third century and repeatedly set forth in creeds and Church-council resolutions, was (and remains) an article of Roman Catholic faith. But in modern times it had been supplied with loopholes, largest among them a "baptism of desire" whereby righteous non-Catholics could be deemed "in" the Church through imputation of an implicit desire to belong to it. Even Pope Pius IX, the nineteenth-century exemplar of uncompromising Roman Catholicism, kept the gates of heaven open to the unprofessed. In the United States, successive Baltimore Catechisms assured American Catholics that their non-Catholic fellow citizens were not necessarily consigned to eternal damnation. Feeney's insistence that they were indeed so consigned was nevertheless based on good, if pre-modern, authority; to read the texts is to conclude that some of the Church fathers, popes, and councils had meant what he claimed. When his followers asked their teachers at Boston College, Holy Cross, and Emmanuel for a simple affirmation of the dogma, and received qualifications instead, they were filled with dismay. Liberalism was taking over the Church.

The sense of beleaguerment grew. When a number of Jesuits who were studying at Harvard began showing up at the center to contest his views, Feeney, who regarded their very presence in Harvard classrooms as an affront to the faith, banned them from the premises. He also ceased having guest speakers in from outside, saying that they would only be a distraction now that St. Benedict's had started to develop its own spirit and point of view. Not all of the students who frequented the center were prepared to go along. Young Robert F. Kennedy, for one, took exception to what was being taught and, going home, distressed his mother by denouncing Feeney at the family dinner table.[6] But then there was Temple Morgan.

Morgan was the epitome of Fair Harvard: scion of an old Harvard family, captain of the boxing team, member of the premier private club, the Porcellian. A flier during the war, he had returned to complete college in a state of spiritual unrest. Dissatisfied with his courses, at a loss as to what to do, he took to watching from across the street as Feeney delivered his Thursday-night allocutions. Before long he was drawn into the life of the center; and on Easter Sunday of 1947, in the last semester of his senior year, Temple Morgan had himself baptized into the Roman Catholic Church. A few days later he moved out of his rooms in Lowell House, withdrew from Harvard College, resigned from the Porcellian Club, and matriculated at St. Benedict Center. The shock waves reverberated through Harvard's upper crust. A dean, who happened to be a relative of Morgan's, called on Feeney, but received merely a testimonial to the young man's nobility and integrity. Other relatives began placing phone calls to the archbishop and the Jesuit provincial. Members of the Boston hierarchy and the Society of Jesus found themselves invited to dine where they had never dined before. The Corporation, Harvard's chief governing body, discussed the affair. Rome itself heard about it.

Aware of complaints about Feeney when he visited the center in October of 1947, Archbishop Cushing may not have heard of its distinctive theology, although it was beginning to be criticized at St. John's, the archdiocesan seminary. The criticism was known to John Wright, the clever intellectual who was now Auxiliary Bishop of Boston and Cushing's right-hand man. But Wright had every reason for wanting to get the archbishop's enthusiastic support for St. Benedict's on record, lest he, as the center's original sponsor in the hierarchy, take the fall when push came to shove. Cushing, in fact, was not one to sympathize with Feeney's theological hard line. Born and raised in South Boston, the nursery of Boston Irish politics, he possessed a good politician's warmth, shrewdness, and feel for cultural diversity. Deeply impressed by the happy marriage of one of his sisters to a Jewish man he liked, he was, in particular, a strong opponent of anti-Semitism. On becoming archbishop in 1944, he determined to make a break with the style of his predecessor.

Cardinal O'Connell, though personally given to hobnobbing with the non-Catholic Back Bay gentry, had been a staunch "Romanist" who never missed the opportunity to thump the drums of Catholic separatism. He frowned on Catholic boys' going to Harvard and forbade absolution for sins to Catholic mothers who placed "the education and care of their children in the hands of infidels, heretics, and atheists"—that is to say, who sent them to secular schools—"for merely social reasons." Cushing, by contrast, began acting the ecumenist long before it became fashionable for Catholic prelates to do so, appearing at interfaith gatherings like the Massachusetts Committee of Catholics, Protestants, and Jews (where in 1945 he preached religious tolerance and love of neighbor "irrespective of race, creed, or color"). In "Catholics and Communism," the first of his contributions to *From the Housetops*, Cushing warned against thinking of the case against Communism as "an exclusively *Catholic* one," pointing out that "although Red Fascism threatens us Catholics and our institutions, it threatens with equal violence and fatal purpose all others who love God or seek to serve Him."[7]

Nineteen forty-eight rolled around, and with the shouts from the housetops louder than ever, the Boston hierarchy decided the time had come to put some distance between itself and St. Benedict Center. In February, the archbishop made a speech calling for an end to feuding over religious dogmas. "We cannot any longer," he said, "afford the luxury of fighting one another over doctrines concerning the next world, though we must not compromise these. We are faced with a situation in which all men of good will must unite their forces to save what is worth saving in this world."[8] The following month, Bishop Wright appeared at a meeting of the Harvard Liberal Union to state the Catholic case against universal military training. Feeney and his followers were appalled that a Catholic prelate should appear on the podium, and even curry the favor, of an organization which stood for all they considered noxious in the world. And then, just after Spring Break, Cushing came to High Table.

His host, House Master Perkins, had been closely touched by the defection of Temple Morgan. Not only had Temple resided at Lowell, but Perkins had been his academic tutor, and knew his father. Perkins, whose own father, a prominent Boston attorney, had for many years been Senior Fellow of the Harvard Corporation, was a thoroughbred Brahmin. As far as he was concerned, Feeney was preaching war, and the archbishop had to be brought into the picture. Always at pains to observe the proprieties, he prohibited his senior common room from raising the subject—and arranged for a Catholic undergraduate to be seated on either side of the guest of honor. When he observed one of them speaking about the business at hand, Perkins apologized. "That's all right," replied the archbishop. "I brought it up myself." For the rest of the meal, and on into the night over brandy and cigars in the master's residence, discussion raged over Father Feeney, the activities of St. Benedict Center, and the question of salvation outside the church. Before being invited to Lowell House, Cushing said, he had received letters about what was going on. He did not know much about it. A lot of what he was hearing was news to him. He had once spoken at the center, but he would speak anywhere. He was not sure he approved of its methods. It wasn't true that only professed Roman Catholics could be saved. He would investigate. The occasion concluded on the most amicable terms, with the archbishop suggesting that a High Table invitation be extended to his subordinate, Bishop Wright, who unlike himself was a real scholar.

The next day found Harvard Yard abuzz with Cushing's visit, and St. Benedict's in a frenzy of alarm. That the archbishop of Boston had discussed the center and its activities in the very belly of the beast could only signify a threat to its very existence. A delegation was dispatched to Brighton to meet with Bishop Wright, but finding him not at home, it went directly to His Eminence. Cushing confirmed the impression of his encounter with Lowell House, said not to believe rumors about the center's closing, and suggested that the person to see about such matters was his auxiliary bishop. Wright himself was furious that the group had gone over his head. In two successive meetings he expressed reservations about the center's approach to non-Catholics, stressed the importance of obeying one's parents, and insisted that the center was in no danger. But the vise was closing. On August 8, speaking at St. Columban's Seminary, Archbishop Cushing announced that if any Catholic organization was harboring prejudices against Jews or other non-Catholics, "I will assume the responsibility of remedying it."[9] A week later, he and Wright were on the high seas, bound for Rome on a pilgrimage to promote the beatification of Pope Pius X. On the twenty-fifth, John J. McEleney, the Jesuit provincial of New England, instructed Father Feeney by letter to report for duty to Holy Cross College in Worcester on September 8. Feeney protested in vain, and the pleas of his flock were likewise unavailing. Bags packed and car waiting, he held a climactic meeting with St. Benedict's inner circle. The competing claims of Truth and Obedience were hung in the balance, and Truth proved the weightier. Liberal Catholicism would go unchallenged in America if St. Benedict Center went Feeneyless.

Through the fall, Feeney refused all efforts to budge him from his course. In November, Evelyn Waugh, visiting Boston, encountered an embarrassed reticence from the local Catholics he questioned about the recalcitrant Jesuit—"a saint & apostle on no account to be missed," according to what Mrs. Luce had told him. "I went one morning by appointment," Waugh wrote his wife, "& found him surrounded by a court of bemused youths of both sexes & he stark, raving mad. . . . He fell into a rambling denunciation of all secular learning which gradually became more & more violent." When Feeney began to attack Ronald Knox, the English Catholic luminary of whom his guest was both friend and admiring biographer, Waugh blew up. "His court sat absolutely aghast at hearing their holy man addressed like this. And in unbroken silence I walked out of the house. . . . It seemed to me he needed an exorcist more than an alienist. A case of demoniac possession & jolly frightening."[10] Just after Christmas, Feeney was informed by McEleney that his priestly faculties would not be renewed; he was no longer permitted to perform the sacraments. In January, he constituted his followers as a religious order, called the Slaves of the Immaculate Heart of Mary.

Meanwhile, several adherents of the center who taught at Boston College began to feel the heat. Two members of the philosophy department, David Walsh and Fakhri Maluf, were haled before the college president and questioned closely about Father Feeney and St. Benedict Center. Maluf, an implacable hard-liner, had acquired a reputation for flunking students who disagreed with him. Refusing to alter his course on Aquinas, he charged the graduate school with teaching heresy and was promptly dropped from its faculty. Throughout the archdiocese, Catholic theologians were up in arms over the question of salvation outside the Church. In January, the theology department of Boston College circulated a four-page "position statement" on the subject by Philip J. Donnelly, professor of dogmatic theology at Weston. Donnelly attacked *From the Housetops* by name, contending that the formula *extra ecclesiam nulla salus* "must not be understood in the sense that salvation is impossible for anyone who does not believe explicitly in the Catholic Church, and does not accept all the revealed truths proposed by her for belief." On February 11, St. Benedict Center wrote the Pope complaining that the "insidious heresy" of salvation outside the Church was receiving official Catholic approval in the United States. Two weeks later, a letter was sent to the general of the Society of Jesus accusing Jesuit-sponsored BC of heresy. About the same time, Feeney refused a second order to report to Holy Cross, this one issued by his old teacher Vincent McCormick, assistant to the Jesuit general, who had been sent from Rome to settle the affair. On April Fools' Day, after an exchange of letters, the two met at Boston College. Standing on conscience, Feeney demanded that the Society make a public declaration of the reason for his transfer. McCormick demurred, and before returning to Rome directed that any of Feeney's followers teaching at a Jesuit institution be required to sign Father Donnelly's statement. Three BC faculty members refused, and were fired. Another Feeney loyalist, who taught at the Boston College High School, was let go for the same reason.

The "Boston Heresy Case" broke in the middle of Holy Week. The four firings were front-page news, and not only in Boston. In New York, the *Times* began a series, and the story was picked up by *Time, Life,* and *Newsweek* as well. On Good Friday, Feeneyites, as they came to be called, took up positions outside Boston's churches, holding placards and hawking the latest number of *From the Housetops,* which was entirely given over to a polemic against the Donnelly statement. The salvation of non-Catholics was soon being discussed in Boston bars and on Boston street corners. Cabbies catechized any fare with a clerical collar. Such lay concern with doctrine was unheard of in American Catholicism. If anything, it recalled the Arian controversy of the fourth century, when the streets of Constantinople were loud with argument over the substance of the person of the Son of God.

The day after Easter, Archbishop Cushing silenced Father Feeney. "Weighty points of dogma," he declared, "are not debated in headlines nor made the occasion of recrimination and inordinate attack on constituted authority." Revealing that Feeney had already been deprived of priestly functions, the archbishop denied Catholics frequenting or assisting St. Benedict Center "the right to receive the Sacrament of Penance and the Holy Eucharist." But the center held firm. War was waged in the press and protest lodged with all available authorities. Feeney himself took to showing up Sundays on the Boston Common to proclaim his views. His insistent cry was for an *ex cathedra* (which would mean infallible) pronouncement from the Pope. While he never received that, there did arrive a letter from the Holy Office, issued August 8, which explicitly condemned the St. Benedict interpretation of *extra ecclesiam nulla salus.* It stated that though "all Catholics are bound in faith" to the dictum, a person could be united to the Church by no more than "implicit desire."[11] The same day, Feeney was informed that proceedings were under way to dismiss him from the Society of Jesus.

The dismissal came on October 28. Four years later, after refusing under pain of excommunication to appear before ecclesiastical examiners in Rome, Leonard Feeney was formally excluded, for indiscipline, from the Roman communion. By then, the Slaves of the Immaculate Heart of Mary had become an outlaw band on the fringes of American Catholicism. Anathematized by Church authorities, their school deprived of accreditation, they supported themselves by selling their leader's devotional works to unsuspecting Catholics on hit-and-run forays into parishes around the country. Occasionally they would be arrested or hustled out of town for vending without a license. In 1953, a group of Feeneyites made the AP wire by getting into a scuffle at Notre Dame. "The first sign of your approaching damnation," one had declaimed, "is that Notre Dame has Protestants on its football team."

Every Sunday, the Slaves assembled on Boston Common to hear Feeney denounce his enemies: Protestants, Masons, the Boston hierarchy, and especially the Jews. Accompanied by two beefy bodyguards, he would turn on bystanders; hecklers he denounced with accusations of sexual perversion and the classic litany of anti-Semitic invective. In 1955, when Jewish-sponsored Brandeis University, with Cushing's active support, erected a Catholic chapel on its campus, the Feeneyites caused a couple of minor riots in downtown Boston. "We Catholics are . . . being asked," their handbill read, "to approve a scheme whereby Our Lord will be turned over to that people which for 2000 years has rejected, sneered at, reviled, and desecrated Him in the Blessed Sacrament. Catholics of Boston: In the name of the Immaculate Mother of God, this must not happen!"

Finally, in 1957, under pressure from local building inspectors for code violations, Feeney and some one hundred followers left Cambridge for the rural community of Harvard, Massachusetts. There, on a farm next to the site of Bronson Alcott's nineteenth-century transcendentalist commune, Fruitlands, and not far from an old Shaker village, they disposed themselves into a double monastery. All members, including the dozen or so married couples, took vows of celibacy; men and women resided in separate quarters. Children were raised collectively, barely knowing the identity of their parents, under the strict discipline of Mrs. Clarke and a group of the women known as "The Angels." From the accumulation of relics to the most high-flown neoscholastic theologizing, no element of conservative Catholic culture was neglected. Like other tiny species in the American religious bestiary, the Feeneyites discovered that the best way to ensure their purity was to wall themselves off from the rest of society.[12]

"Comic-opera heresy" was how Cushing's biographer described the Feeney affair in 1965. In the full flush of Vatican II, the hysterical hatemonger of Boston Common seemed no more than a pathetic reminder of the buried past—"a nightmarish anachronism, dead upon the vine."[13] Cushing, by contrast, had become an heroic figure: fund-raiser and builder extraordinaire, prince of the Church who was also man of the people, pastor of a martyred president, American ecumenist who had electrified a great Church council with interventions in behalf of religious liberty and the Jews. He, like his beloved "Good Pope John," emblemized the Church making its peace with the modern world. Yet in the late forties, some might have wondered whether it was toward the little-known archbishop of Boston or toward the well-known Jesuit poet that the soul of the Church was more inclined.

Pius XII's famous 1943 encyclical *Mystici Corporis* had harked back to late medieval and Counter-Reformation ecclesiology in equating the Roman Church with the "mystical body of Christ," and this view was reiterated in both Rome's letter on the Boston College case and the encyclical *Humani Generis* (1950). It effectively made membership in the institutional Church a requirement for salvation, for in classical Christian thought, Christ's mystical body signified all of the saved. Worthy pagans, Jews, and heretics could therefore be granted the possibility of salvation only on the ground that they were (unwitting) Roman Catholics, incorporated by unconscious longing or desire into the One True Church's visible body. The encyclicals were in fact directed against some of the very theologians whose more ecumenical ideas on the nature of the Church were to win out at Vatican II. Thus, in hoping for a rigorist enunciation of *extra ecclesiam nulla salus,* Feeney was simply sailing before the prevailing Roman winds. He had, in the words of one commentator, "merely drawn the scholastic theology to its logical conclusions."[14]

In general, the Church had no use for the ecumenical movement of the time, energized in the first assembly of the World Council of Churches in Amsterdam in 1949. The Vatican forbade Catholics to attend the assembly even as observers; communicants received a strict injunction to explain Roman Catholic teaching "whole and entire" and to make clear that "true reunion could come about only by the return of dissidents to the one true Church of Christ."[15] In the Holy Year 1950, the Virgin Mary's bodily assumption into Heaven was proclaimed official Church doctrine: one more course was added to the Marian wall separating Catholics and Protestants. That was precisely in line with the piety of the Slaves of the Immaculate Heart of Mary.

In place of ecumenism, the Church offered a vision of integral Catholicism that had entranced American Catholic leaders between the two world wars. Theirs was not simply a religion, but an entire culture possessed of art, literature, and above all a philosophical system (neo-Thomism) capable of integrating all knowledge. To bring this message of unity home to the faithful, a wide range of Catholic movements and professional societies sprang into being. Social and liturgical reformers stressed the corporate ideal of Catholic life. In 1939, Catholic educators were for the first time urged to go beyond mere catechetical instruction and provide undergraduates with courses in theology itself, the queen of the sciences. In October, 1946, a new magazine called *Integrity* announced in capital letters: "WE MUST MAKE A NEW SYNTHESIS OF RELIGION AND LIFE."[16] St. Benedict Center was nothing if not an example of this synthesis in action.

The conversionist ideology operating strongly within

American Catholicism was, in some measure, a defensive response to a new social reality. As American Catholics began to move from immigrant enclaves into the mainstream of a great pluralist society, how was the Church to hold on to them? The answer was to foster separate institutions and a separate view of the world. Yet this ran the risk of reinvigorating the old charge that Catholicism was alien to the spirit of America. And it was against that charge that Cushing took his stand, in speech after speech, during the late forties. Catholicism was not opposed to freedom, he told a meeting of the Holy Name Convention in 1947; Catholics wanted American principles as much as anybody. "Give no man ground to attack Catholicism because of your imperfect Americanism," he warned the Manchester, New Hampshire, Knights of Columbus. "Demonstrate, for all to see, that to be a good *Catholic* is to be a good *American* and that to be a *Catholic American* is to be the best, the happiest, the most loyal person in this world or the next." To be sure, he admitted to Marquette's 1948 graduating class, history bore witness to the danger of identifying religion and patriotism, but in America just the opposite threatened: "the danger of so divorcing spiritual morality and secular loyalty that the latter loses its only effective sanctions and therefore disintegrates and dies." America needed Catholicism, he told the Holy Namers in 1946, to serve "as one of the greatest bulwarks against the inroads of Communism." And the anti-Communist cause required good relations with people of other faiths. "Part of the Red Fascist plan," he informed a 1947 convention of the Knights, was "to pit religious groups against one another, to divide Christians one from the other." For that reason, at least in part, "I promised when first I became Archbishop to desist from all argument with our non-Catholic neighbors and from all purely defensive talks about Catholicism."[17]

Argument with non-Catholic neighbors was exactly what Leonard Feeney had in mind, and he was not about to sacrifice it on an altar of patriotism. "Here in America," he told a reporter, "instead of religion we talk about 'good Americanism' and 'The Constitution of the United States.' Why, sometimes I believe that the people of this country believe Americanism is more important than religion!" The characteristic religious expression of Americanism was that relatively new institution, the interfaith meeting: "a place where a Jewish rabbi, who does not believe in the divinity of Christ, and a Protestant minister, who doubts it, get together with a Catholic priest, who agrees to forget it for the evening." What the country really needed was the bluntest possible insistence that the only true church was the Catholic Church. "That sounds like a cruel regime, but it isn't. What is really cruel is to deny others the knowledge of where salvation really is." [18]

Interfaith conflict did not disappear after the war; thanks to growing Catholic self-confidence—and consequent Protestant fears of growing Catholic "power"—it seemed at times to be on the rise. In 1952, intense Protestant lobbying succeeded in putting an end to the ambassadorial appointment to the Vatican that Franklin Roosevelt had initiated in 1939; and through the Truman and Eisenhower administrations, there was heavy political skirmishing over the issue of federal aid to parochial schools. But such conflict took place within stricter rhetorical bounds than ever before. In order to be presentable to the postwar public, religion needed to gird itself in the robes of adhesion. Anything less was imperfect Americanism—and above all when it came to Communism. The week the Boston Heresy Case broke, the front pages announced the fall of Nanking before the red armies of Mao Zedong. Having made their own headlines, the Feeneyites found fellow Catholics accusing them of aiding the enemy by creating division among America's spiritual forces. They protested that eternal damnation was an even greater threat to humankind than Communism. [19] It was a protest that fell on deaf ears.

5 ■ WARS OF FAITH

``T O D A Y there is less communication between great groups of men than there was in the roadless world of a thousand years ago. We can no more communicate with half of mankind than we can raise the dead. The while the anti-Christ stalks our world. Organized communism seeks even to dethrone God from his central place in the Universe. It attempts to uproot everywhere it goes the gentle and restraining influences of the religion of love and peace. One by one the lamps of civilization go out."[1] Thus did the darling of the liberal intelligentsia, Adlai Stevenson, chat from the fireside to the American people a month before the 1952 elections. Admittedly, the normally dry and restrained Democratic presidential candidate was running against an opponent given to public pieties; and he also needed to make clear, in the face of McCarthyite attacks, that his party was just as orthodox in its anti-Communism as the GOP. Yet how readily the language of spiritual combat came to his lips. It is not easy to exaggerate the religious dimension of America's cold-war sensibility, or the extent to which Communism called into play the country's adhesional faith.

Among the stewards of the religion of love and peace,

Roman Catholics led the alarums. Catholic anti-Communism was of long standing; to progressives who remembered the Church's support of General Franco during the Spanish Civil War, it was notorious. But the establishment of Communist governments in Eastern Europe, especially in Poland, lent new urgency to the Church's pronouncements. In the struggle with atheistic Communism, warned the Pope in 1947, "even a few minutes can decide the victory." American bishops mounted campaigns against the persecution by Communist authorities of Hungary's Cardinal Mindszenty and Yugoslavia's Cardinal Stepinac. The American Catholic press, in the late forties, made anti-Communism its number one concern. Not that Americans needed to be convinced that Communism was against religion. According to a 1947 Gallup Poll, 72 percent of them believed that the Communists would destroy the Christian religion if they could. Another poll, taken two years later, had 77 percent denying that someone could be both a good Christian and a member of the Communist Party. So much, in fact, did Communism seem the enemy of religion that even the red-hunters in Congress were forced to back off when they set out to uncover it in the churches.[2]

Given the atmosphere of the time, mainline Protestantism was vulnerable; for while very few Protestant clerics were either actual Communists or apologists for the Soviet Union, numbers of them had enlisted in organizations dedicated to peace, international understanding, and social justice which would later make the attorney general's list of subversive bodies. Nevertheless, Chairman Harold Velde of the House Un-American Activities Committee kicked up a storm of protest in March of 1953 when he let drop the remark that the committee was thinking about investigating several church groups and a handful of clergymen. In the course of defending the committee against the mounting criticism, Congressman Donald Jackson of California charged one of the main critics, the Methodist bishop of Washington and Protestant panjandrum G. Bromley Oxnam, with being "to the Communist front what Man O'War was to thoroughbred horse racing." Jackson then made public papers purportedly documenting Oxnam's front activities. Oxnam, in reply, published a point-by-point rebuttal of the charges in *The Washington Post* and went on to debate Jackson on the "American Forum of the Air," where he demanded the right to appear before the committee to set the record straight. On July 21, under the glare of television lights and to massive press coverage, he faced the committee down, eliciting a unanimous declaration that it had "no record of any Communist Party affiliation or membership by Bishop Oxnam."[3] On the other side of Capitol Hill, meanwhile, Senator Joseph McCarthy was receiving his own first comeuppance, again over a matter of clerical red-baiting.

The accuser in this case was J. B. Matthews, a classicist and theologian who as a young man had been a radical of many parts: Methodist missionary and supporter of Indonesian nationalism on Java, teacher and ardent integrationist at black colleges in the South, pacifist leader and warrior against capitalist influence over Protestant churches in New York City. In the late thirties, however, Matthews abandoned his leftist ways and became a scourge of the left, serving as director of research for the House Un-American Activities Committee from 1938 to 1945. After the war he continued this work freelance, and on June 22, 1953, Senator McCarthy appointed him executive director of his Permanent Sub-Committee on Investigations. Less than two weeks later, the July number of *The American Mercury* was on the newsstands with Matthews' "Reds and Our Churches" as its featured article. "The largest single group supporting the Communist apparatus in the United States today," proclaimed the lead, "is composed of Protestant clergymen." At least seven thousand of them were "party members, fellow-travelers, espionage agents, party-line adherents, or unwitting dupes"—all serving a cause which aimed at "the total obliteration of Judeo-Christian civilization." It was "nothing short of a monstrous puzzle." Without indicating precisely how he had arrived at his figure, Matthews furnished an array of names, beginning with those of eight Episcopal bishops, gleaned from various petitions and organization membership lists. Why, he wanted to know, should clergymen be immune from the scrutiny directed at professors and federal bureaucrats?[4]

Outrage and indignation rained down on Washington.

Senator McCarthy enjoyed the enthusiastic support of many of his fellow Roman Catholics. Wasn't this nothing less than a Catholic anti-Protestant campaign? In fact, McCarthy had always been at pains to dress his crusade in ecumenical garb, as when he told the editors of America in 1950 that Communism sought to destroy "all the honesty and decency that every Protestant, Jew and Catholic . . . [had] been taught at his mother's knee." Now, with a majority of his subcommittee demanding it, Matthews would have to go. At the White House, a group of anti-McCarthy presidential assistants, led by liberal Catholic speechwriter Emmett John Hughes, began frantic efforts to get what would be Eisenhower's first direct attack on McCarthy into the hands of the press before the junior senator from Wisconsin could break the news of Matthews' dismissal. Working closely with the National Conference of Christians and Jews in New York, which wanted White House support for its own denunciation of McCarthy, they arranged for an exchange of telegrams: one from the NCCJ protesting the Matthews article and the other expressing Ike's concurrence. Both reached the wire an hour ahead of McCarthy's announcement.

Signed by the organization's Catholic, Jewish, and Protestant cochairmen—Monsignor John A. O'Brien of Notre Dame, Rabbi Maurice Eisendrath, president of the Union of American Hebrew Congregations, and the Reverend Dr. John Sutherland Bonnell, pastor of New York's Fifth Avenue Presbyterian Church—the NCCJ telegram called Matthews' article "unjustified and deplorable." Congress had the right to investigate the loyalty of any citizen, but "destroying trust in the leaders of Protestantism, Catholicism, and Judaism by wholesale condemnation is to weaken the greatest American bulwark against atheistic materialism and communism." In his response, which Hughes drafted, the president stated that he fully shared "the conviction you state," and concluded by enunciating three interlocking propositions: "The churches of America are citadels of our faith in individual freedom and human dignity. This faith is the living source of all our spiritual strength. And this strength is our matchless armor in our world-wide struggle against the forces of Godless tyranny and oppression." Obviously, the Communists knew exactly what they were doing when they made war on religion.[5]

Yet why did it seem so important to make religion the safeguard of the American democracy? Behind the commonplaces of cold-war rhetoric lurked worries that democratic values and institutions were in themselves not very strong, certainly not in the face of a determined threat. The collapse of the European democracies before fascism remained vividly in mind, and the counterevidence of subsequent Allied triumph was ambiguous. World War II "has not vindicated democracy as against totalitarianism—not with Russia coming out of it the principal victor," wrote the Protestant journalist Paul Hutchinson. "Is a return to religion necessary," asked the *Partisan Review* symposium on religion and the intellectuals, "in order to counter the new means of social discipline that we all fear: totalitarianism?" Even those who refused to draft religion into the antitotalitarian service betrayed a sense of democracy's shortcomings in the inspiration department. "What we need as a rallying cry," cried Sidney Hook, "is freedom, not salvation." An anxiety to make freedom our "fighting faith" likewise animated *The Vital Center*, Arthur Schlesinger, Jr.'s, manifesto for the new liberal political organization Americans for Democratic Action. Its opening chapter, "Politics in an Age of Anxiety," announced that Western man was "tense, uncertain, adrift." The new (1949-style) liberalism was, said Schlesinger, more sober than the old, more realistic for having been unburdened of the illusion that social progress was inevitable. The great need now was simply to find a way to protect free society short of war, and the first step in doing so was to understand more clearly "*why* free society has failed."[6]

Something had gone wrong with our nation, wrote John Foster Dulles in 1950, "or we should not be in our present plight and mood." It was not like us to be "on the defensive" and "fearful." The trouble was not material; what we lacked was a "righteous and dynamic faith." True, our influence and security were in decline while the Soviet Union's were on the rise. But, though the Red Army constituted a "background threat," this was not primarily because Russia had become a great military power. It was because Soviet Communism had "a creed . . . of world wide import . . . in which the hard core of Party members believe fanatically, and which they are spreading with missionary zeal throughout the world." Democracy, wrote Will Herberg, "cannot serve as our saving faith"; it needed to be grounded "in something more ultimate, in some really total commitment that will protect it from inner corruption as well as from external attack." Only "prophetic faith" would enable us to resist "the dynamism of totalitarianism." When it came to dynamic faiths, the advantage seemed all on the other side.[7]

Late in 1945, Secretary of the Navy James Forrestal had commissioned a study of the moral and philosophical foundations of the Soviet state, because, as he explained to Walter Lippmann, "to me the fundamental question in respect to our relations with Russia is whether we are dealing with a nation or a religion." That Communism amounted to a religion was not a new thought, but in the years after the war it received wholesale elaboration and endless reiteration. In a 1948 volume, *Communism and the Conscience of the West*, the prolific Fulton Sheen laid out a sequence of Catholic doctrines, from the Trinity to the sacraments, and showed Communist analogues to each one. On the Protestant side, the case was made in such books as Alexander Miller's *The Christian Significance of Karl Marx* (1947), John Bennett's *Christianity and Communism* (1948), and William Hordern's *Christianity, Communism and History* (1954). Hordern, a former student of Bennett's at Union, conveyed the common message in no uncertain terms. The "real power and appeal of Communism lie in its promise of an essential meaning to the history of man. . . . It gives meaning to living in the present and hope for the future." Jesus Christ and Karl Marx had both founded new religions, and "today these two religious systems face each other in the world. No other force can rival them." So "if we lose the struggle with Communism, it will not be because we have been outproduced: it will be because we have been less dedicated and less inspired by our religious faith than the Communist world."[8]

Former Party members testified to the religious character of Communist allegiance. In 1949, a number of leading literary ex-Communists contributed essays to a volume called *The God That Failed*; the authors (grouped into "initiates" and "worshippers from afar") were at pains to point out that although the Communist deity had failed them, he was succeeding only too well with their erstwhile coreligionists. Those prodigals who came back to the Judeo-Christian God were the greatest heroes. A Bill Mauldin cartoon from 1947 shows a scruffy young couple sitting under a portrait of Stalin. "Two magazines are competing for exclusive serial rights," says the man, "if we convert." Louis Budenz, a prominent Communist journalist during the thirties, wrote an account of his reversion to Roman Catholicism in which he compared himself to Saint Augustine, who had spent nine years in thrall to the Manichees before going back to the faith of his mother. Elizabeth Bentley, the confessed espionage agent known to the tabloids as the Red Spy Queen, also transferred her loyalty to Catholicism. "People who are genuine Communists, as I was, aren't the lukewarm type," she told reporters. "They can't go into a vacuum if they give up Communism. They must have something to tie to." For passion and celebrity, however, no one could compete with Whittaker Chambers.[9]

Chambers had played an important role in the American Communist apparatus before the war, serving ultimately as chief courier for Bentley's espionage operation in Washington. In the late thirties, disgusted at the Soviet purges, he broke with the Party and, after a year out in the cold, managed to secure a job at *Time* magazine. A writer of talent as well as a bona fide intellectual, he prospered in Luceland and quickly rose to the position of senior editor. He also tied onto religion, first having himself baptized and confirmed in the Episcopal Cathedral of St. John the Divine, and later joining the Society of Friends. When, in 1948, he testified that a onetime shining knight of the New Deal, Alger Hiss, was also a onetime Soviet spy, he became one of the great controversial figures of the day. *Witness*, his 1952 autobiography, was a tale of conversion both to and from Communism, and it was filled with admiration for those he had fled. In a spiritually diseased Western society, the Communists were "that part of mankind which has recovered the power to live or die—to bear witness—for its faith." The only possible answer to their challenge was a faith of equal power. God was the sole "inciter and guarantor" of Communism's opposite, freedom; indeed, freedom and religion were indivisible. In the West, political freedom was merely a political reading of the Bible. "At every point religion and politics interlace, and must do so more acutely as the conflict between the two great camps of men—those who reject and those who worship God—becomes irrepressible."[10]

But how could religion and politics be so interlaced as to meet the Communist challenge? Reinhold Niebuhr plumped for the Judeo-Christian conception of human nature. Asserting that Communism and secular liberalism were comparably deluded, he argued that if we could only "understand that the evils against which we contend are frequently the fruit of illusions which are similar to our own, we might be better prepared to save a vast uncommitted world, particularly in Asia, which lies between ourselves and communism, from being engulfed by this noxious creed." J. Paul Williams, chairman of the religion department at Mount Holyoke, went so far as to suggest adhesional public policy. In "The Role of Religion in American Destiny," the last chapter of his widely used textbook on religion in America, he endorsed the "widespread" opinion that American dedication to the democratic way of life was "insufficient to carry through the crises of the coming decades"; the peril, he said, was increased by the "religious fanaticism" of Communism's "devotees," which stood in stark contrast to our own inattention to the "spiritual core" of our national existence. What was necessary was for Americans to regard the democratic ideal as the Will of God, or at least as the Law of Nature; democracy had to be made no less than "an object of religious dedication." The churches and synagogues could not bear full responsibility for this. "The state must be brought into the picture; governmental agencies must teach the democratic ideal as religion." That meant both "ceremonial reinforcement" and "metaphysical sanctions . . . open indoctrination of the faith that the democratic ideal accords with ultimate reality, whether that reality be conceived in naturalistic or supernaturalistic terms." [11]

This was too much for *The Christian Century*'s reviewer, who wrote that the old faiths, not the "Established Democratic Church of America," would be the answer "if totalitarianism comes to America under the name of democracy." The conservative thinker Ernest Van Den Haag also rejected democracy as an adequate political religion. A democratic dogma could hold its own against "the rival secularized eschatologies" only at the expense of freedom and democracy itself. Any society that wished to avoid totalitarianism needed to ensure its stability with real religious sanctions, a "transcendent myth." Whether or not such myths happened to be true was of no social or political consequence. "It matters only that they are believed," he wrote. Godly or secular, true or false, some sort of believable faith was required to stem the onrushing totalitarian tide. Intellectuals might debate its nature and how it was to be instilled. Outside the study, the issue looked a good deal less complicated. [12]

That the American people as a whole were looking to faith as a mighty fortress is perhaps indicated by their promotion, between 1942 and 1947, of religious leaders from third (after government and business leaders) to first place as that group "doing the most good for the country." (Indeed, over the next decade the proportion of those who thought so increased from 32.6 to 46 percent.) Among this body of public benefactors the Reverend Peter Marshall was exemplary. His story was the stuff of American myth: a pious Scots boy of humble means who comes to the United States and makes good, gaining fame and influence commensurate with his deserts. Marshall rose to become pastor of the New York Avenue Presbyterian Church, the first ecclesiastical edifice in the nation's capital and the one "where Lincoln worshipped." Before dying prematurely of a heart attack in 1949, he also served two years as chaplain of the U.S. Senate, where his pungent invocations were said even to delight the ears of the cynics in the press gallery. His widow, Catherine, as literary torchbearer, turned some of his prayers and sermons into a 1949 best-seller; and she included more of them in an even better-selling biography, *A Man Called Peter*, which, after gracing the top of the nonfiction list in 1952, became a movie starring Richard Todd. Marshall's messages to the Senate, though nonpartisan, were hardly unpolitical. "The particular concept which he longed to give his Congressional flock," wrote Mrs. Marshall, "was that God was not only concerned about American policy, but that he could tell the individual legislator how to vote. It was not that Peter wanted to influence legislation; but he did want God to have the chance to influence it." And conceivably vice versa.[13]

On Sunday, February 7, 1954, the President and Mrs. Eisenhower were sitting in the Lincoln pew when Marshall's successor, the Reverend George M. Docherty, made bold to recommend an official acknowledgment of the Lord's sovereign concern for the affairs of the United States. Docherty, like Marshall, was a Scottish émigré, and in pondering the daily inaugural rite of his adopted nation's schools he had come to "a strange conclusion." There was something missing in the Pledge of Allegiance, "and that which was missing was the characteristic and definitive factor in the American way of life. Indeed, apart from the mention of the phrase 'the United States of America,' it could be the pledge of any republic. In fact, I could hear little Moscovites [sic] repeat a similar pledge to their hammer-and-sickle flag in Moscow with equal solemnity. Russia is also a republic that claims to have overthrown the tyranny of kingship. Russia also claims to be indivisible." The definitive factor in the American way of life was God Himself. The pledge, said Docherty, should be amended to read "one nation *under God*"—the latter words lifted from that famous American scripture, Lincoln's Gettysburg Address ("that this nation, under God, shall have a new birth of freedom").[14]

The proposed change had actually been kicking around for several years in Roman Catholic circles. In 1951, the supreme board of directors of the Knights of Columbus had, for its assembly meetings, amended the pledge in just that way, and the following year passed a resolution calling on Congress to make it official. But although a Catholic congressman from

Michigan, Louis Rabaut, had introduced legislation to do so in April of 1953, it took a Presbyterian sermon to stir Congress into action. No fewer than seventeen new bills were quickly dropped into the congressional hoppers, one by Michigan's Senator Horace Ferguson, the others by members of the House. Rabaut rose to say that while he and Docherty were not of the same Christian denomination, the Protestant pastor had in this matter "hit the nail right on the head."

A hitch or two developed along the way. On April 5, possibly because of qualms about impinging on the separation of church and state, the Senate Judiciary Committee voted to postpone the Ferguson resolution indefinitely. On May 10, however, after Rabaut had secured a House Judiciary subcommittee's unanimous support for his own resolution, the Senate committee turned around and reported its measure out; and the whole Senate unanimously rendered its approval the following day. By the end of the month the full House Judiciary Committee had done the same. The process was hurried along by an avalanche of mail, evoked by various radio commentators and the Hearst press from thousands of individual citizens and a vast array of veterans' groups, civic and fraternal clubs, patriotic organizations, labor unions, and trade associations. At the very moment when Senator McCarthy's assault on the U.S. Army was grabbing the headlines and filling the television screens, the issue that seemed to touch Americans most closely was the inclusion of God in the Pledge of Allegiance. "An invasion of religious liberty," protested the Association of Unitarian Ministers up in Boston, but theirs was not a voice that many heeded.[15]

Preparations were laid for the president to sign the resolution into law on Flag Day, June 14, whereupon a flag-raising ceremony at the Capitol would culminate the American Legion's new drive to encourage people to fly the Stars and Stripes on all patriotic occasions. Just before final House passage, and to the utter exasperation of his colleagues, Congressman Rabaut refused to allow the already passed (and identical) Senate resolution to be substituted for his own; this flagrant violation of Congressional etiquette could well have prevented the bill from being ready for Flag Day had not Senator Ferguson graciously withdrawn his resolution in favor of Rabaut's. In the event, the amended pledge was officially pronounced for the first time from the steps of the Capitol by Messrs. Rabaut and Ferguson in unison, as Walter Cronkite and the CBS television cameras conveyed the ceremony, "New Glory for Old Glory," across the land. In his remarks at the signing of the bill, President Eisenhower had expressed satisfaction that America's schoolchildren would now be proclaiming daily "the dedication of our Nation and our people to the Almighty." Such avowal of "our country's true meaning" was, he said, especially significant in today's world, where mankind had been "cruelly torn by violence and brutality," where millions had been "deadened in mind and soul by a materialistic philosophy of life," and where all were "appalled by the prospect of atomic war." By reaffirming "the transcendence of religious faith in America's heritage and future" we would be continually strengthening "those spiritual weapons which forever will be our country's most powerful resource, in peace or in war." [16]

Here, in the ritual joining of God and Flag, was prime ceremonial reinforcement of the nation's spiritual core, though perhaps not quite in the democracy-as-religion form that Professor Williams had in mind. In the first Christian centuries, the Church had responded to unwanted new doctrine by recasting its creed, thus creating at once a new heresy and a new orthodoxy; and the pledge amendment amounted to the same thing. "I believe this modification of the pledge is important because it highlights one of the real fundamental differences between the free world and the Communist world," said Senator Ferguson. "You and I know," said Congressman Rabaut, "that the Union of Soviet Socialist Republics would not, and could not, while supporting the philosophy of communism, place in its patriotic ritual an acknowledgment that their nation existed 'under God.' " (By contrast, an atheistic American was, according to the Reverend Mr. Docherty, "a contradiction in terms.") Belief in God, said Congressman Overton Brooks of Louisiana, was the one thing separating "free people of the

Western World from the rabid Communist." By this modification of the pledge, "we in effect declare openly that we denounce the pagan doctrine of communism and declare 'under
God' in favor of free government and a free world." The flood
of mail to Congress in May of 1954 was not, as the *Times*
reporter averred, "on a subject far removed from the Army–
McCarthy hearings." It too concerned the central ideological
preoccupation of the day.[17]

What was it about Communism that impelled this creedal
revision? In the final sermon of his hugely successful 1952
Washington revival, Billy Graham warned that we were a "des-
perately wicked people" whom God would (unless we repented) soon destroy, since He could not "long abide our sins
of materialism." In similar if less impassioned terms, Secretary
of State Dulles, the Presbyterian minister's son, decried the
"materialistic emphasis" of American society, which, he said,
the Soviets themselves cited as evidence that we had adopted
their "materialistic thesis." The greatest American need was to
"regain confidence in our spiritual heritage," to "reject totally
the Marxian thesis that material things are primary and spiritual things only secondary." Communism was thus the ideological incarnation of our own besetting sin. Its temptation,
issued *as* religion, was to live according to the flesh; and to
resist it we needed to embrace the traditional remedy of repentance and return to God. "Our nation has long recognized
that if we are to survive this challenge of materialism, of sel-
fishness, of immorality, it will only be with the help of a power
greater than our own," declared Congressman Oliver Bolton of
Ohio. As usual with American foreign policy, the moral dynamic was domestic.[18]

In 1954, Congress required all U.S. coins and paper currency to bear the slogan "In God We Trust," and two years
later that became the official U.S. motto, winning out over "E
Pluribus Unum." There was even an effort to get more specific.
In the month of all the pledge fever, the Senate Judiciary Sub-
committee on Constitutional Amendments held hearings on a
proposal by Senator Ralph Flanders of Vermont to amend the
Constitution to recognize the authority and law of Jesus Christ.

The only elected official to show up, however, was the sub-committee chairman, William Langer of South Dakota; Flanders himself did not bother to testify. This "Christian Amendment," as it was called, had been offered many times in the course of more than a century, and prospects for passage now were as dim as ever. The representatives of a united front of Jewish groups, testifying against the bill, had no trouble carrying the day.

Adhesional religious symbolism was what Congress wanted, not invidious distinctions among the God-fearing. "Let us join together, Protestant, Jew, and Catholic, in taking this action," asked Congressman Peter Rodino of New Jersey in behalf of the pledge amendment. In the great postwar war of faith, there might be interservice rivalry among the several faiths, but all were fighting on the same side. In 1955, an undenominational prayer room was created in the Capitol, its design worked out with the advice and consent of the two (Protestant) congressional chaplains, the assistant chancellor of Washington's Roman Catholic Archdiocese, and the rabbi of the Washington Hebrew Congregation. The following year, Congress ordained that all first- and second-class mail be cancelled with a die bearing the equally undenominational message "Pray for Peace." Given "the ever increasing attacks upon us by forces of godlessness and atheism," it was well to be reminded of "our dependence upon God and of our faith in His support," declared the bill's ever-zealous sponsor, Congressman Rabaut. And of course, our supplication would be made known "to the four corners of the earth." [19]

But what did these adhesional emblems, these pledges and mottoes and prayer rooms and cancellation dies, have to do with "real" Judeo-Christianity? What about the prophetic exposure of society's false absolutes and sanctimonious self-righteousness? If that was what the Judeo-Christian tradition was really about, then its theological promoters were duty-bound to take up arms against the public religiosity of the day. And so they did, belaboring the Fourth Great Awakening with neo-orthodox cudgels in a series of well-received books: Roy Eckardt's *The Surge of Piety in America* (1958), Martin Marty's *The New Shape of American Religion* (1959), Peter Berger's

The Noise of Solemn Assemblies (1961). Indeed, these books, together with Will Herberg's *Protestant Catholic Jew*, established the portrait of American religion in the fifties that we carry around today. "Authentic Jewish-Christian faith," wrote Herberg, had less to fear from "overt and avowed unbelief" than from the secularized piety of "the contemporary religious revival." [20]

Yet the neo-orthodox had problems of their own. In promoting Judeo-Christian prophetism and joining the ideological fray, they were, after all, bearing their own adhesional witness; and as such were faced, like other leaders of the postwar revival, with the dilemma of urging profound, unsecularized faith on a religiously plural collective. Diverse were the perils of spiritual consensus-building in postwar America. If for neo-evangelical revivalism they lay in a congenital readiness to celebrate the country, for neo-orthodoxy they lay in a congenital unease with special salvific claims on behalf of one or another version of the common faith. That unease was nowhere more apparent than in the guerrilla action that Reinhold Niebuhr mounted against Billy Graham, when enthusiasm for the evangelist within the Protestant establishment was at its height.

Niebuhr fired first from his own journal, *Christianity and Crisis*, in a March 5, 1956, editorial responding to news that Graham would be coming to lead a crusade in New York City the following year. "We dread the prospect," he wrote.

> Billy Graham is a personable, modest and appealing young man who has wedded considerable dramatic and demagogic gifts with a rather obscurantist version of the Christian faith. His message is not completely irrelevant to the broader social issues of the day but it approaches irrelevance. For what it may be worth, we can be assured that his approach is free of the vulgarities which characterized the message of Billy Sunday, who intrigued the nation about a quarter century ago. We are grateful for this much "progress."

The central charge was that by "presenting Christianity as a series of simple answers to complex questions" Graham would only strengthen the modern inclination to dismiss the Gospel as irrelevant to contemporary life.[21]

Niebuhr's editorial "we," however, presumed too much, for two issues later there appeared in the journal's letters column a sharp rejoinder from his fellow editorial board member and boss, Henry P. Van Dusen, the president of Union. Calling such opposition to Graham "thoroughly unscriptural" for ignoring apostolic recognition of "diversities of gifts" and "differences of operations," Van Dusen emphasized the need to present the masses with a "more readily digestible form" of the Gospel than the " 'strong meat' of a sophisticated interpretation."

> Dr. Niebuhr prefers Billy Graham to Billy Sunday. There are many, of whom I am one, who are not ashamed to testify that they would probably never have come within the sound of Dr. Niebuhr's voice or the influence of his mind if they had not been first touched by the message of the earlier Billy. Quite probably five or ten years hence there may appear in the classrooms and churches of Billy Graham's severest critics not a few who will be glad to give parallel testimony to his role in starting them in that direction.

Simple answers had their time and place.[22]

Niebuhr, unpersuaded, next carried the attack to the pages of The Christian Century, where in May he rather more gently took Graham to task for biblical literalism and pietistic moralism. In a mannerly reply, E. G. Homrighausen, dean of Princeton Seminary and head of the National Council of Churches' Department of Evangelism, called Niebuhrian neo-orthodoxy "hesitant and weak in calling persons to a positive faith."

> I have, frankly, been disappointed in its inability to lead the way in the revival or rebirth or restoration of a relevant Protestantism in the local church. And if men like Graham have arisen and are being heard by the thousands, it may be that what he is and says in sincerity ought to be said in a better way by the neo-

orthodox with all their accumulation of intelligence about the Bible and history and personality in our times.

Niebuhr, in August, came back with a "Proposal to Billy Graham," which urged Graham to raise high the banner of racial justice "and become a vital force in the nation's moral and spiritual life." This inspired the Baptist theologian E. J. Carnell to issue "A Proposal to Reinhold Niebuhr" urging the dialectical theologian to let his "Yes" to Billy Graham resound ("dialectically") as loudly as his "No." [23]

Niebuhr's softening tone toward Graham was in accord with the importunate note that crept into establishmentarian discourse in anticipation of the impending crusade. Preparations for it, said *The Christian Century*, were "so extensive that they threaten to overrun every other church activity." Those questioning it "beg for a diversified campaign so that a fuller, more accurate account of Protestant Christianity will be given the great community." Granted that the big money would be withdrawn if Drs. Niebuhr, Tillich, or Bennett were featured "even in smaller tents [!]," might not Dr. Graham be "more explicit about his ecumenicity"? [24] The fear was that it was the establishment, not the Gospel, that Graham would be rendering irrelevant in Gotham. In the event, the NCC's Department of Evangelism jumped on the bandwagon; H. H. McConnell, the deputy executive director, assumed responsibility for directing the follow-up program of "visitation evangelism." But even before Graham stood up to address his first Madison Square Garden crowd on May 15, 1957, the bloom was coming off the rose for the department's executive director, Berlyn Farris.

In early 1955, not long after he took office, that revival enthusiast had persuaded NCC leaders to create a commission to study the need and place of evangelism in contemporary Protestantism, and its role in the work of the National Council of Churches. The twenty-three member commission included Farris and some of his staff as consultants, and featured such disparate figures as E. G. Homrighausen, Georgia Harkness, and Norman Vincent Peale; but the actual writing was turned over to Yale's Robert Calhoun, a man of distinct neo-orthodox sympathies. Not surprisingly, the report, presented at the NCC General Board meeting on May 1 and 2, 1957, embodied a barely disguised neo-orthodox critique of the whole American revivalist tradition.

Original sin, it held, condemned society for all time to the status of "a living corporate web of wrong action and impulse that no human being can escape." The evils of the day were not faithlessness and bad morals but the idols of a modern civilization more complex than what went before. Evangelism was the business of God and the entire Church; though preachers possessed a special role, the itinerant exhortation of mass audiences was an uncertain thing.

> Such preaching is revivalism, a method that involves both possible values and very real perils for evangelism, to which it can at best make substantial contributions, of which at worst it can be a gross caricature, and with which in any event it is not to be identified. Revivalists can indeed, under God, be evangelists of power; but it is not their distinctive method that makes them so.

According to the minutes of the meeting, various suggestions were offered toward making the document more conventionally evangelical. One discussion group "asked for a more positive description of revivalism as it relates to evangelism." (In the final, printed version, the phrase "possible values and very real perils" was changed to "possible values and possible perils.") Yet nowhere was there either the rallying cry or the organizational detail that Executive Director Farris had originally had in mind. A week later, in his report to the managers of his department, he bravely called the report "stimulating, challenging, and thought-provoking," adding: "It won't answer all the questions, but it will build fires under our thinking." A month later, citing the department's intractable shortage of funds, he suddenly announced his resignation, effective July 1, to become director of district evangelism for the Board of Evangelism of the Methodist Church.[25]

But what really turned the tide in Niebuhr's favor was the revival itself. As *Life* described it on July 1, "Billy Graham opened his New York crusade in high hopes that it would 'soon be like a mighty river through the city.' But after 37 days of his 66-day stand in Madison Square Garden, the river has not been mighty. New Yorkers have talked surprisingly little about Billy—unlike his smash hits in London and Los Angeles, where he was the talk of the town." Graham was not the force to be reckoned with that had been hoped, and feared. Moreover, the actual look of the revival, with its well-oiled mechanisms of conversion, its well-scrubbed and well-mannered audiences, helped bring about a new view of Graham, evident in *The Christian Century's* three stiff editorials on the crusade but put most bluntly in a piece contributed to *Life* by Niebuhr himself:

> Graham is honest and describes the signers of his decision cards as "inquirers" rather than "converts." It would be interesting to know how many of those attracted by his evangelistic Christianity are attracted by the obvious fact that his new evangelism is much blander than the old. For it promises a new life, not through painful religious experience but merely by signing a decision card. Thus a miracle of regeneration is promised at a painless price by an obviously sincere evangelist. It is a bargain.

The long-term effects of Graham's revivals had previously been questioned, but in contrast, say, with Peale, he had always been credited with offering up the good, strict old-time evangelical faith. Now he was merely part of the pious scene, purveying the things of the spirit on the cheap.[26]

Billy, for his part, turned the other cheek. "I have read nearly everything Mr. Niebuhr has written, and I feel inadequate before his brilliant mind and learning," he told journalist Noel Houston. He continued his pursuit of good but not overclose relations with the NCC. In December of 1957, for example, he wrote to General Secretary Roy G. Ross expressing thanks that his greetings had been extended to the Council's General Assembly; apologizing for not being able to attend in person ("due to extensive dental work and one or two speaking commitments"); applauding the choice of Edwin Dahlberg as president ("I have admired him for many years"); and mentioning his recent collaboration with the Department of Evangelism's H. H. McConnell ("a very warm friend"). As far as the Protestant establishment was concerned, however, New York was Graham's high-water mark. After that there were no more expectations that revival à la Billy might, for better or worse, actually make a difference.[27]

Profound religion, real religion—that was the desideratum. In 1958, in what is surely one of the few *Life* articles ever to make its way into the scholarly footnotes, Henry P. Van Dusen identified a "Third Force" in Christianity (alongside Catholicism and Protestantism) composed of Adventists, Pentecostals, Jehovah's Witnesses, and other often-despised "fringe" groups; growing by leaps and bounds, this force was no less than "the most extraordinary religious phenomenon of our time." Van Dusen had first become aware of the phenomenon while spending three months in the Caribbean three years before. Now he celebrated its "direct biblical message," describing the promise of "an immediate, life transforming experience of the living-God-in-Christ" as "far more significant to many individuals than the version of it normally found in conventional churches." He stressed, above all, that followers were expected "to practice an active, untiring, seven-day-a-week Christianity."

Sympathetic enough to the new evangelicals to have served on Billy Graham's New York committee, Van Dusen nonetheless drew no connection between the Third Force and the National Association of Evangelicals, though five of the Third Force groups listed at the end of his article—the Assemblies of God, the Church of God (Cleveland, Tennessee), the International Church of the Foursquare Gospel, the Pentecostal Church of God in America, and the Pentecostal Holiness Church—in fact constituted nearly two-thirds of the NAE's total membership. It was as though the NAE *as such* had become too conventional, as though the vitality of the Third Force had to lie in its distance from any sort of religious consensus. In *The New Shape of American Religion*, Martin Marty took more or less this tack. After blaming Billy Graham for his "failure to become unpopular with people outside the churches," he turned to the "protesting intransigents" of the Third Force: "The square pegs that do not fit the round holes of eroded religious expression might call us all to a higher witness." [28]

But what would that witness be? By the end of the decade Reinhold Niebuhr was willing to grant that the West had been successfully inoculated against Communism "by the historical dynamism of the Judaeo-Christian tradition." Meanwhile, he stunned the Protestant theological community when, in a paper before a joint meeting of the faculties of the Jewish and Union Theological seminaries, he pronounced Judaism and Christianity "sufficiently alike for the Jew to find God more easily in terms of his own religious heritage than by subjecting himself to the hazards of guilt feeling involved in a conversion to a faith, which whatever its excellencies, must appear to him as a symbol of an oppressive majority culture." [29] Profound faith as common cause—adhesion through conversion—was becoming too hard an act; as the cold war faded, some new middle term was needed to keep the two in balance. The Social Gospel of an earlier day had combined deep piety with public witness. In turning the corner of the 1950s, the medium for adhesional faith would once again be social action.

6 ■ WHO SHALL OVERCOME

O N February 20, 1960, the lunch-counter sit-ins which had begun three weeks earlier in Greensboro, North Carolina, reached Nashville. That day all was quiet: the counters simply shut down when the demonstrators appeared. A week later, however, bands of white youths appeared on the heels of the students from Fisk University, the American Baptist Seminary, and Tennessee Agricultural and Industrial University—the local black institutions of higher learning. The whites taunted, spat upon, and crushed lighted cigarettes out on the backs of the black students, but there was no fighting back. Instead, the students sang (for the first time in the civil rights movement) an old labor-union song called "We Shall Overcome," and gave their assailants a textbook demonstration of the techniques of passive resistance. These they had learned from a young black Methodist minister named James M. Lawson, Jr.[1]

Formerly vice-president of the National Conference of Methodist Youth, the tall, soft-spoken Lawson was a pacifist who had gone to prison rather than serve in the Korean war. Paroled to the Methodist Board of Missions, he had been sent to India, where he learned about Gandhian passive resistance and witnessed its fruits at first hand. In 1958, as the civil rights movement was gathering force, Lawson left the Oberlin School of Theology in his native Ohio and headed down to Nashville, enrolling there in Vanderbilt University's divinity school, the most intellectually exciting seminary south of the Mason-Dixon line (and long closely associated with the Methodist Church). His field placement was as a paid representative of A. J. Muste's pacifist Fellowship of Reconciliation, and it was in this capacity that, in his senior year, he prepared the students for the sit-ins.

On February 29, Mayor Ben West called a meeting with black church leaders to discuss the municipal crisis that the lunch-counter campaign had precipitated. Toward the end of the meeting, Lawson offered a point-by-point rationale for the sit-ins and indicated that he would continue to support civil disobedience against the local Jim Crow ordinances. (The law, he said—or was at least widely quoted as saying—had been "a gimmick to keep the Negro in his place.") The mayor lost his cool, and he was not the only one. The *Nashville Banner*, the city's highly conservative evening paper, charged the young minister with "contemptuous challenge of civil authority" and "incitation to anarchy." At Vanderbilt, Chancellor Harvie Branscomb instructed J. Robert Nelson, the dean of the Divinity School, to inform Lawson that (under a rule devised the year before in response to a series of undergraduate panty raids) the university forbade students to take part in any sort of mob action. On March 2 (Ash Wednesday, as it happened), Branscomb convened the executive committee of Vanderbilt's governing Board of Trust, a body which included James G. Stahlman, owner and editor of the *Banner*, and John E. Sloan, whose department store contained one of the lunch counters in question. Dean Nelson, who had worked closely with Lawson drafting statements to counteract the press accounts, argued that nonviolent protest was neither lawlessness nor anarchy but fully consistent with Christian ethics. Ignoring Nelson's plea to take no disciplinary step, the committee decided to ask Lawson to withdraw from the university because of his advocacy of civil disobedience; when he refused to do so, Branscomb went ahead and ordered him dismissed.

At the divinity school, it was like tapping a keg at a temperance rally. Immediately, the students pledged themselves to support their classmate, calling his expulsion "a grave error" and "a violation of Christian conscience." Hardly had faculty members, meeting on March 4, themselves resolved to protest the chancellor's action when word came that Lawson had been arrested, and that downtown Nashville was in an uproar. Checks were written, a legal-defense fund agreed upon, and a group of professors, led by the dean, proceeded to the jail, paid the $500 bail, and drove the accused home. On March 8, the faculty of the Vanderbilt Divinity School formally requested the reinstatement of student James Lawson. In violation of normal procedures, he had been given no opportunity to confront his accusers; nor had its own prerogatives in matters of student discipline been respected. Lawson was the best of the four black students at the divinity school, and these were the only four blacks enrolled in the entire university. Broadly sympathetic to the civil rights movement, the divinity faculty was not about to acquiesce quietly in the resegregation of Vanderbilt.

The rest of the university was less up in arms; indeed, both the student newspaper and the student senate indicated their support of the executive committee's decision. And while a quarter of the university's other faculty was mustered to sign a statement in support of Lawson, the faculty senate, an advisory body chaired by the chancellor, went no further than to appoint a committee to look into procedures which could be applied in future cases. For his part, Chancellor Branscomb was not a dyed-in-the-wool racist; it was under his leadership that the divinity school had admitted its first black student in 1953—a year before, as the university in later years liked to note with pride, the U.S. Supreme Court declared public-school segregation unconstitutional. The university's own dining hall was, as Branscomb pointed out in a self-justifying letter to The Christian Century, "not a segregated institution." This small measure of integration went hand in hand with his efforts to make Vanderbilt into a school of national caliber—upgrading graduate and professional schools, constructing new dormitories to increase the number of out-of-state students. A progressive stance on race was by now *de rigueur* for a ranking American university.

But Vanderbilt remained an institution of and by the local conservative gentry, and the idea that it was from within this bastion of gentility that trouble had come to Nashville was in the highest degree infuriating. The chancellor, himself an Alabamian, saw the incident as a threat to the social order. Turning "civil disobedience" into a shibboleth, he declared again and again that it was this principled commitment to flout assertedly unjust laws, and not the mere participation in demonstrations, that had put Lawson beyond the pale. Branscomb was, to boot, a distinguished New Testament scholar who, before assuming the chancellorship, had been dean of the divinity school at Duke; he was not about to let a bunch of self-righteous theologians pull moral rank on him. "The word 'conscience,' " he wrote to *The Christian Century*, "is not a talisman which by itself will solve these [complex social] problems." [2]

From his standpoint, the timing could not have been worse. A few years earlier, John D. Rockefeller III's Sealantic Fund had seen fit to treble the divinity school's endowment, and Vanderbilt had in consequence shelled out $1.3 million to build the school a new chapel and quadrangle; the dedication ceremonies were scheduled for March 21. On the seventeenth, the divinity faculty was outraged to learn that it would have to wait two months—until the next meeting of the full Board of Trust—before presenting its case in the Lawson matter. Not surprisingly, the dedication turned into a public relations nightmare for Branscomb. His handling of the Lawson case was condemned by a number of the distinguished guest speakers, including Dean Lister Pope of the Yale Divinity School, who stated flatly: "Only the expression of opposition by students and faculty of the school has served to preserve the reputation of this university among its sister institutions." In addition, one hundred fifty alumni, on hand for the occasion, passed a resolution supporting the faculty and calling for Lawson's reinstatement. Wags suggested that the quadrangle had been dedicated not to the school's late dean but to the dismissed Reverend Mr. Lawson.

Through the spring the case festered, a *cause célèbre* not only in the pages of *The Christian Century*, which accorded it editorial after editorial, but across the state of Tennessee. Lawson became a star of the civil rights movement; "the young people's Martin Luther King" they called him, though he was not much younger than King himself. With the university showing no sign of backing down, a majority of the divinity faculty, some of whom had from the first hinted at resignation, began casting about for non-Vanderbilt futures. The man in the middle was J. Robert Nelson. Not yet forty, he was a golden boy of the postwar ecumenical movement, having served as executive secretary of the World Council of Churches' Faith and Order commission; when he came to Vanderbilt in 1957, Nashville welcomed him with open arms. While standing up for Lawson, Nelson had at the same time labored for a compromise; but the irenic spirit which reigned in Geneva was not so easily applied to racial tension in the American South. Nashville society closed its doors, Branscomb turned the coldest of shoulders, and the divinity faculty itself lost confidence in its embattled dean: if he wasn't Branscomb's man, then neither was he theirs.

In the meantime, the sit-in campaign more or less achieved its end with the integration of seven Nashville lunch counters. None of the eighty students arrested for breaking the law had been prosecuted, nor was there any indication that they would be. Among the demonstrators were two dozen white Vanderbilt students, against whom the university itself had taken no action. Thus, by the time of the May 21 meeting of the Board of Trust, Vanderbilt was far out on a limb in the matter of James Lawson. Nevertheless, and despite some impassioned pleading from within, the board decided not to permit Lawson to return. There followed, in the days surrounding commencement weekend, an intensified protest which culminated on May 31, when the dean and ten of the school's sixteen professors resigned; three new graduates returned their degrees; and seventeen students quit, among them the three remaining blacks. The crisis was now real. Powerful support for the divinity school arrived from other departmental quarters: physics, chemistry, speech, the social sciences, and, most importantly, from the medical school, the university's pride and joy. It had become clear that the chancellor was prepared to dissolve his seminary—there was talk about what to do with the buildings—but losing the medical faculty was something else again. Branscomb and Harold Vanderbilt (president of the Board of Trust and the only non-Nashvillian on the executive committee) therefore accepted a settlement which would have both permitted Lawson to come back to prepare for his three final exams and returned all resignations: in effect, a total surrender. When the executive committee rejected it, renewed faculty protest finally persuaded the chancellor to accept, on the authority that had always been his, the stated terms—short only of reinstating the dean.

Lawson himself, claiming that the agreement was vague as to exactly how he would receive his degree and unfair in placing the onus of blame on Dean Nelson, did not go back to Vanderbilt. (He accepted an offer to complete his degree over the summer at the Boston University School of Theology, Martin Luther King, Jr.'s, alma mater.) But the student resignations were all withdrawn, including those of the three blacks, who stated their belief that the case had been settled "honorably" and that they could return "with dignity and self-respect." All the faculty members returned as well, except for one who had in the interim accepted a job elsewhere. And so the Lawson story, having flashed coast-to-coast in late May and early June, quickly faded from national consciousness. By fall, any lingering institutional stigma proved insufficient to prevent the Ford Foundation from making Vanderbilt one of five American universities to receive multimillion-dollar matching grants. Hard feelings were vented only by the spurned Nelson, who in August wrote a long account of the episode for *The Christian Century* in which he suggested that the nine returning faculty members had abandoned the cause in the delusion that "this development actually constituted a liberal victory."[3] After a year at Princeton and three at Oberlin, he himself followed Lawson's footsteps to Boston University, assuming a chair in systematic theology. Branscomb retired in 1963—a few years earlier, it was generally thought, than he otherwise would have.

In the December 28, 1959, number of *Christianity and Crisis*, John Bennett had bidden farewell to the old decade and welcomed in the new by dilating on the twin spiritual modalities of "prophetic challenge" and "pastoral identification": "The first without the second may lead to a sterile self-righteousness and the second without the first may lead to a betrayal of the Church's mission. There can never be a perfect balance but if in the 1950's the scales were tipped far too much in favor of identification, in the 1960's we should pray and hope for the tipping of the scales in favor of prophetic challenge and criticism." Bennett's prayers and hopes were more than answered, for by decade's end the scales had nearly tipped over from the weight of Judeo-Christian prophetism. At first, however, the balance looked pretty good, and the Lawson episode was a case in point.

Civil rights, the supreme cause of the day, was to a striking degree a religious affair. The name of Martin Luther King, Jr.'s, Southern Christian Leadership Conference simply expressed the reality of an organization dependent on the social cohesion and moral strength which the church provided America's black communities. SCLC volunteers were required to sign a Commitment Card to the nonviolent movement, among whose "ten commandments" were "MEDITATE daily on the teachings and life of Jesus": "WALK and TALK in the manner of love, for God is love"; and "PRAY daily to be used by God in order that all men might be free." His was an "army," wrote King, "whose allegiance was to God."[4]

But it was not just the religion of black people that mattered. If James Lawson did what he did, the faculty, students, and alumni of the nearly all-white Vanderbilt Divinity School also did what they did, and an entire university was led kicking and screaming into the paths of righteousness. In white

America, churchfolk were moving to the front of an issue of social reform in a way not seen at least since Prohibition, and perhaps since the abolitionist crusade itself; at the tail end of the Billy Graham decade, this too recalled the country's evangelical Protestant past. And it was precisely the institutional plushness of postwar religion, deprecated to the point of cliché by so many commentators, that made the central role of the clergy in the civil rights movement, and perhaps the movement itself, possible. For prophets require auditors, and in the fifties the public, churchily complacent or otherwise, was attentive to voices of faith. Yet for the prophetic fire to ignite in 1960, the continued flaying of a smug and suburbanized piety was not enough. Some theological readjustment was necessary; even John Bennett, epigone of neo-orthodoxy that he was, seemed to acknowledge it. Not only had the recent "revival of interest in religious activity" tended to minimize specific Christian witness in favor of assimilating faith to the larger, secular culture; in his view, the concurrent "revival of theology" (in the form of neo-orthodoxy) might have overstressed faith's independence from that broader environment, and thus "not always helped the Church to be relevant in its criticism of culture." Moral man had perhaps resigned himself too readily to immoral society.[5]

A few months into the new decade, as the lunch-counter demonstrations were pushing civil rights to the top of the domestic agenda, the acknowledged leader of the movement made his contribution to The Christian Century's latest How My Mind Has Changed series; and like many of Martin Luther King, Jr.'s, performances, it was artfully carried out. At first, King began, he had been a "thoroughgoing liberal." But then he had read Reinhold Niebuhr, and discovered a deeper view of man's sinfulness: "I came to feel that liberalism had been all too sentimental concerning human nature and that it leaned toward a false idealism." (Whence "the basic change in my thinking.") Yet (he continued) he had never succumbed to an "all-out acceptance of neo-orthodoxy." Though he could not go along with its spiritual optimism, Walter Rauschenbusch's Christianity and Social Progress, the gospel of the Social Gospel, left "an indelible imprint on my thinking": "Any religion that professes to be concerned about the souls of men and is not concerned about the slums that damn them, the economic conditions that strangle them and the social conditions that cripple them is a spiritually moribund religion awaiting burial." But how to embrace this Social Gospel given the neo-orthodox doubt that the power of Christian love could change people's hearts and transform society? He found the answer in Mahatma Gandhi's concept of *satyagraha*—the truth-force or love-force of nonviolent protest. "As I delved deeper into the philosophy of Gandhi my skepticism concerning the power of love gradually diminished, and I came to see for the first time that the Christian doctrine of love operating through the Gandhian method of nonviolence was one of the most potent weapons available to oppressed people in their struggle for freedom." This new understanding had been deepened and strengthened by the actual experience of nonviolent protest: "Many issues I had not cleared up intellectually concerning nonviolence were now solved in the sphere of practical action." From the 1955 Montgomery bus boycott on, *satyagraha*, resolver of neo-orthodox misgivings, became the distinguishing feature of the neo-Social Gospel of Martin Luther King, Jr.[6]

Carefully calculated as it was for its clerical audience, this brief intellectual autobiography (which also included an encounter with existentialism) summed up the theological situation of the moment. Like Bennett's goodbye to the fifties, it conveyed a growing sense that neo-orthodoxy had had its day, that something new was in the air. (At Vanderbilt itself, an influential critique of the whole neo-orthodox enterprise was being mounted by Langdon Gilkey, one of the faculty members who sided with James Lawson.) The great generation of Barth and Brunner, of Bultmann and Tillich, of the Niebuhr brothers, was passing. It was not that these men had been uncommitted on the social issues of the day; far from it. But the theology of man's utter distance from God, of the imperfectibility of human affairs, could not make for a politics of social redemption. The Niebuhrians especially talked again and again of prophecy, but their own prophetic witness had more to do

with the breaking of idols and the exposure of false prophets
than with any summons to a promised land. And it was this
kind of prophetic leadership that the new spiritual politics
required.

In *The Suburban Captivity of the Churches*, a book which
attracted considerable attention when it appeared in 1961,
Gibson Winter took out after fifties-style religion in a wholly
un–neo-orthodox way. Although he had no use for the "organization church" of routinized busyness, his was not a call, à
la Herberg, for deep faith and existential commitment. Indeed,
Winter specifically shunned such ultimacies, passing over
"the beliefs and teaching of the churches" in the conviction
that most current discussion of Protestantism carried an "excessive emphasis on belief and ideology." His concern, rather,
was with the "social embodiment" of religiousness in the very
ecclesiastical forms which, in his view, Protestant leaders both
scorned and spent their lives maintaining. Pastors, he said,
should cease their immersion in the "private sphere of life"
and put their churches to work renewing urban America:
"This interpretation of religious responsibility extends to all
phases of metropolitan development—the ghettos, housing in-
equities, school deficiencies in slum areas, exploitation of
newcomers by real estate and business interests, the disregard
for life that permits residential areas to become highways, and
the inadequate fire inspections in slum areas. The churches
are not alone in this responsibility, of course, but they bear a
large share of the burden."[7] That religion needed to increase
its presence in the world of social action was, in 1960, beginning to be clear to the broad range of politically liberal church-
men. It was not, however, the only message concerning
religion's place in public life that reached their ears in that
presidential election year.

A few weeks before election day, Archbishop James P.
Davis of San Juan and two other Puerto Rican bishops, Luis
Aponte Martínez and James E. McManus, issued a pastoral
letter which instructed their flocks not to vote to reelect Gov-
ernor Luis Muñoz Marín and his Popular Democratic Party.
Himself a divorced Roman Catholic, Muñoz had supported

birth control, tolerated common-law marriage, and opposed religious education. A vote for him, said Bishop McManus, would be a "sin of disobedience." Such clerical intervention was anything but new in the politics of the island, and in the event, Muñoz was enthusiastically returned to office by the overwhelmingly Catholic populace. On the mainland, however, the letter was less easy to shrug off. "If enough voters realize that Puerto Rico is American soil," said presidential candidate John F. Kennedy to his aide Ted Sorensen, "this election is lost."[8]

Within the Kennedy campaign, it did not seem like an isolated incident. Back in May, a few weeks after the candidate had informed the American Society of Newspaper Editors that he would not "be responsive in any way to ecclesiastic pressure or obligations," L'Osservatore Romano insisted that the Church possessed "the duty and right" to "intervene" in the political arena. Was the Church intervening to prevent the election of Jack Kennedy? Suspicion immediately fastened on the Cardinal Archbishop of New York, Francis Spellman. To be sure, after news of the Puerto Rican pastoral letter kicked off the predictable ruckus, Spellman issued a statement suggesting that the island's Catholic voters would not be committing a sin if they disregarded their bishops in this matter. Yet Puerto Rico was a Spellman appanage, and only a week before promulgation of the letter he had been on hand to consecrate Bishop Martínez and install Archbishop Davis. The thought that he had orchestrated the affair was hard to dismiss (though to this day it has never been proved).

In an off-the-record talk in March with Paul Hofmann of The New York Times, Egidio Vagnozzi, the Apostolic Delegate to the United States, had indicated (as Hofmann put it in a memo to Times columnist—and ardent Kennedy promoter—Arthur Krock) that "a sophisticated current among Roman Catholics in the U.S. and in the Vatican feels that a Roman Catholic in the White House at this moment might do more harm than good to the Church." Vagnozzi noted that Al Smith's defeat in 1928 had generated sympathy for the Church; there were more concrete reasons for coolness toward a Kennedy candidacy as well. The hierarchy had a political agenda which included (at the symbolic end) the sending of a U.S. ambassador to the Vatican and (at the material one) federal aid to parochial schools. Even doughty Harry Truman had been forced to beat a retreat on the former; and the latter, a subject of considerable recent litigation, was if anything hotter to handle. Candidate Kennedy said he opposed both. He could scarcely have done otherwise. It didn't take very much sophistication to see that his election would bring the hierarchy little immediate tangible gain. Not, of course, that an American bishop would come right out against him. Cardinal Spellman, though, privately indicated his support for Vice President Richard Nixon, and appeared in public with both Nixon and President Eisenhower. (Billy Graham, a Nixon supporter as well, did little more.) Spellman had known and approved of the vice president since the Hiss affair, and he disliked the Kennedys personally, especially father Joe. He was also only too well aware that the special standing he had long enjoyed with American presidents would come to an end if Jack Kennedy was elected. (Archiepiscopal rival Richard Cushing, recently elevated to cardinal, in fact took Spellman's accustomed place of honor at the 1961 inaugural.) Nor did Church politics and Spellman's *amour propre* exhaust the grounds for Roman Catholic disquiet with the junior senator from Massachusetts.[9]

In a March, 1959, article in *Look* on the likelihood the Democrats would run a Catholic for president the following year, Kennedy had been quoted to the effect that should he decide to seek the presidency he would have to make clear where he stood on the church–state issue. This had not sat well with the Jesuit editors of *America*. Didn't the Constitution declare, they asked, that "no religious test shall ever be required as a qualification to any office or public trust under the United States"? And hadn't Kennedy "submitted himself, in effect," to such a test? What bothered them—and a host of other Catholic editors—even more, however, was Kennedy's assertion that "whatever one's religion in his private life may be, for the office-holder nothing takes precedence over his oath to uphold the Constitution and all its parts." Snapped *America:* "Mr. Kennedy doesn't really believe that. No religious man, be he Catholic, Protestant or Jew, holds such an opinion. A man's conscience has a bearing on his public as well as his private life." The senator was no less a Catholic for taking the stands he did on aid to education and the Vatican ambassadorship, said the *St. Louis Review.* "But when he infers that his religion, which teaches him to know, love and serve God above all things and to love his neighbor as himself, will not be allowed to interfere with his oath to the Constitution, it is the Constitution that ought to be examined, not his religion." [10]

In his zeal to calm non-Catholic nerves, Kennedy had, in a sense, no more than passed up the rhetorical armature that American politicians normally girded on. There was no mention of a divine source of guidance, of the Judeo-Christian underpinnings of democracy; his "theme," as *Look* put it, was that "religion is personal, politics are public, and the twain need never meet and conflict." Some Protestant intellectuals were themselves taken aback. To Martin Marty, Kennedy was "spiritually rootless and politically almost disturbingly secular"; to Robert McAfee Brown, he seemed "a rather irregular Christian." [11] Sneer as one might at piety along the Potomac, it was something else again to find a politician hustling religion off the streets. Yet if religion was supposed to play a part in the conduct of the country's business, wasn't the electorate permitted, even obligated, to scrutinize the faith a politician professed? What *about* the constitutional proscription of religious tests for office? And if some concerns were legitimate, how could they even be raised without giving fuel to the bigots? Into this thicket, in May of 1960, plunged the redoubtable G. Bromley Oxnam.

The Methodist Bishop of Washington, besides having served as chairman of his church's Council of Bishops, president of the Federal Council of Churches, and president of the World Council of Churches, was also prominent in Protestants and Other Americans United for the Separation of Church and State, an organization which had mobilized opposition to the various items on the Roman Catholic political agenda. Oxnam was, nonetheless, on cordial terms with Senator Kennedy, and when Sorensen approached him about devising a public statement against bigotry shortly before the May 10 West Virginia primary, he agreed to help. West Virginia, with few Roman Catholics and many conservative Protestants, was a place for Kennedy to prove that he could overcome the religious issue. Together with Dean Francis B. Sayre, Jr., of Washington's Episcopal cathedral, Oxnam assembled a baker's dozen Protestant leaders to sign an "Open Letter" urging their "Fellow Pastors in Christ" to preach "charitable moderation and reasoned balance of judgment." Their homiletic punch line was to be that, in the present campaign anyway, invidious religious distinctions were not to be drawn. "We are convinced that each of the candidates has presented himself before the American people with honesty and independence, and we would think it unjust to discount any one of them because of his chosen faith." A copy of the letter went to every Protestant minister in West Virginia.[12]

But that same week (in its May 10 number, in fact), Look ran "A Protestant View of a Catholic for President," which comprised a series of editorial questions answered jointly by Oxnam and the no less prominent Presbyterian, Eugene Carson Blake. "How do you feel about a Catholic candidate for President?" it began. "Uneasy," they replied. "This uneasiness arises from a feeling, widespread among American Protestants, that the election of a Roman Catholic to the Presidency would both symbolize and strengthen the growing and direct political influence that the Roman Catholic Church exerts on our government and our society." The two wanted to know how a Catholic president would "square his political duties" with his church's views on aid to parochial schools, public access to birth-control information, and the separation of church and state. They shrank before the prospect of the chief executive of the United States kissing a bishop's ring. ("We feel an American President should kneel before no one but God.") Nonetheless, they insisted they would consider voting for a Catholic presidential candidate. "Our votes are not dictated by our religious principles, or by our church. We do not believe that any American's vote should be." [13]

The Look interview certainly seemed at odds with the open letter; where the letter had asked that candidates be chosen "quite apart from what our attitude toward the Roman Church may be," just such an attitude had made for the interviewees' uneasiness. Still, both texts insisted on distinguishing religion from electoral politics. A religious organization might seem threatening, and Oxnam for one did not scruple to take up arms against it in the public forum. But to reject a candidate for being an adherent was a horse of a different color. In the sacred space of the American voting booth, the communion was person-to-person between citizen and candidate, with no dictation from either religious institutions or even religious principles. That, at any rate, was the theory. Whatever hold it had on the voters of West Virginia, whatever effect Oxnam's various pronouncements may have produced in them, they gave the Catholic Kennedy three votes for every two they gave the Protestant Hubert Humphrey. The result, however, did not lay the religious issue to rest.

Was there, in fact, real reason to believe that the Roman Catholic Church might pose some kind of threat to the American polity if one of its members were elected president? As Catholic commentators never tired of pointing out, American Catholics had served their country loyally and well from its beginnings. For that matter, a glance at Western history would have disclosed that even during the Catholic middle ages the number of Western heads of state who had "taken orders from Rome" was tiny. Yet there happened to be a large and authoritative body of Roman Catholic political theory which did not regard the American Constitution's proscription of an establishment of religion as the best of all possible worlds. On the contrary, it held the ideal state to be a Roman Catholic entity which extended its protection to the "one true church" and made sure that non-Catholics did not attempt to proselytize in behalf of their own false faiths. [14]

It was from this theoretical transgression against adhesional Americanism that the most influential anti-Catholic polemic of the postwar period, Paul Blanshard's *American Freedom and Catholic Power* (1949), took wing. Nor was the theory, as Blanshard's critics liked to charge, merely the unattended stuff of theological manuals. Postwar Catholicism, as we have seen, did not embrace religious pluralism; in the late 1950s, John Courtney Murray himself was forbidden by his Jesuit superiors to publish his more pluralistic vision of religion in civil society. Bigotry and cant there were aplenty during the 1960 campaign, but much as Catholic spokesmen insisted on American Catholics' support *in practice* for the separation of church and state, they could not deny that their church demurred from it *in principle*. No Constitutional principle, perhaps, engaged American sensibilities more deeply, and from the outset Kennedy knew that he would have to be seen embracing it with all his might. "The Senator's desire," wrote Sorensen, "was to state his position so clearly and comprehensively that no reasonable man could doubt his adherence to the Constitution." [15]

On the evening of September 12, Kennedy stood up in the ballroom of the Rice Hotel in Houston to address that city's ministerial association. With the presidential campaign in full swing, he would need to respond to the bill of particulars leveled against him by a newly formed organization of prominent conservative Protestant clergy—the National Conference of Citizens for Religious Freedom—whose spokesman was none other than Norman Vincent Peale. (Kennedy, ran its public statement of September 7, could not be free of his church hierarchy's "determined efforts . . . to breach the wall of separation of church and state." [16]) "I believe," said the candidate, "in an America where the separation of church and state is absolute—where no Catholic prelate would tell the President (should he be Catholic) how to act, and no Protestant minister would tell his parishioners for whom to vote." The speech was masterly, and the speaker no less masterly in responding to questions from the floor. For those who had followed his remarks on the religious issue, most of what he had to say was familiar, but there was one significant novelty: "If the time should ever come—and I do not concede any conflict to be remotely possible—when my office would require me to either violate my conscience, or violate the national interest, then I would resign the office, and I hope any other conscientious public servant would do likewise."

That very day, one hundred Protestant, Catholic, and Jewish leaders had issued a "Statement on Religious Liberty in Relation to the 1960 National Campaign" which covered, in a few more words, the identical ground: "No citizen in public office dare be false either to his conscience or to his oath of office. Both his conscience and his oath impose responsibilities sacred under the law of God. If he cannot reconcile the responsibilities entailed by his oath with his conscience, then he must resign, lest he fail his nation and his God." This injunction—or, in Kennedy's case, pledge—was the best the 1960 campaign could muster to solve its spiritual conundrum. If, as the Massachusetts senator had told *Look* the year before, nothing could take precedence over the officeholder's oath to uphold the Constitution, then nothing could take precedence over conscience either. Admitting this allowed for the possibility (however remote) that a president's religion and his constitutional obligations might clash, and afforded a means of resolution which did not subordinate one to the other: resignation.

Kennedy, according to Sorensen, had sought "to still those Protestant critics who were certain he would succumb to pressure and those Catholic critics who were certain he would stifle his faith." [17] Among the former, as analysis of the election returns made clear, there were many who either did not believe him, or did not want to. But Kennedy's Rice Hotel performance effectively drove the religious opposition underground, where, despite a mass of scurrilous propaganda (and the windfall of the Puerto Rican pastoral letter), it went down—if barely—to defeat. Kennedy had told the Houston ministers that an American president's religious views had to be "his own private affair"; what most non-Catholics seemed to want from their newly elected chief executive was precisely the assurance that he would keep his Roman Catholicism to himself, and in that he was happy to oblige. In fact, President Kennedy did not eschew the all-purpose spiritual rhetoric he had skirted when pursuing the office. In his inaugural address, he spoke of his country's ongoing struggle around the world for "the belief that the rights of man come not from the generosity of the state but from the hand of God"; and he concluded by urging his fellow citizens to "go forth to lead the land we love, asking His blessing and His help, but knowing that here on earth God's work must be our own." Yet the Kennedy style was a far cry from what had gone before. In the wake of the missionaries Eisenhower and Dulles came the pragmatic New Frontiersmen, for whom a vigorous secularism was sufficient unto the day.

What *was* the place of religion in American public life? At the beginning of the new decade, the country's spiritual politics seemed at odds with itself, as JFK sent packing to the wings what Martin Luther King had brought to the center of the national stage. From a secular standpoint, to be sure, the civil rights movement and the election of a Roman Catholic to the presidency were about the same thing: removing barriers to full participation ("regardless of race, color, or creed") in American life. Religion, as such, could be seen as no more than instrumental to this comprehensive goal, to be pressed into service or decommissioned as the case demanded. But actually the spiritual politics was of a piece. The postwar religious entente, wherein differences were set aside in order to combat the common totalitarian foe, now turned its attention inward, to the country's unfinished domestic business. Of course no Protestant, Catholic, or Jew could be barred from office, if there was nothing exclusionary in his religious identification. Faith was on the march as prophetic challenge, and it was a challenge for the entire community. The Judeo-Christian tradition had come home to roost.

In the middle of January, 1963, a conference was convened at Chicago's Edgewater Beach Hotel by the Department of Racial and Cultural Relations of the National Council of Churches, the Social Action Commission of the Synagogue Council of America, and the Social Action Department of the National Catholic Welfare Conference. Six hundred fifty-seven delegates from these and sixty-seven other religious and religiously affiliated groups turned out for four days of speeches and workshops. Marking the one-hundreth anniversary of Lincoln's Emancipation Proclamation, the National Conference on Religion and Race was neither one more exercise in "interfaith dialogue" nor, like the National Conference of Christians and Jews, ecumenism at the periphery. For the first time in the history of American religion, central bodies of Protestantism, Catholicism, and Judaism had joined for the purpose of spearheading a nationwide social reform—specifically, "to increase the leadership of religion in ending racial discrimination in the United States."[18] It was something very like a new American religious establishment.

The Roman Catholic presence was formidable. Led by Chicago's Cardinal Meyer, twenty-five bishops and archbishops—not to mention assorted lower clergy and members of religious orders—actively participated; the executive director was Mathew Ahmann, who headed the National Catholic Conference for Interracial Justice. Chicago was the home of liberal Catholicism in America, but more looked to be afoot than Chicago liberalism; Balfour Brickner, the director of Interfaith Activities for Reform Judaism's Union of American Hebrew Congregations, judged that the extent of the hierarchy's involvement "may be indicative of a significant departure in Catholic non-Catholic relationships." Only a month before, the first two-month session of the Second Vatican Council had concluded, and Cardinal Meyer, in his address to the conference, brought word of a new spirit aborning in Rome. The council, he said, had invited "all men of good will" to work to establish "a more ordered way of living and greater brotherhood" in this world. Interracial justice was "a joint work and a glorious work. May our common Father in Heaven bless our efforts." The actual pronouncements of Vatican II were, of course, yet to come, and Brickner was himself unprepared to say whether a "fresh wind" was really "beginning to blow through the atmosphere of inter-religious relations" as a whole. Of increased Catholic collaboration in interreligious civil rights lobbying, however, he had no doubt.[19]

The conference went about as well as its conveners could have wished. The delegates repeatedly acknowledged that the many mansions in their Father's house were themselves beset with racial prejudice and exclusiveness, and they called for integrating all religious functions and for adopting nondiscriminatory policies across the ecclesiastical board. From self-scrutiny, they proceeded outward; churches were to serve as examples to other organizations, as educators of the wider public, as pursuers of racial justice in the courts and legislatures of the land. And to cap the specific recommendations, there issued an Appeal to the Conscience of the American People to eradicate racism ("our most serious domestic evil") "with all diligence and speed," and "to do this for the glory of God." It was a glory in which all bathed. "Kinship in God" is the "underlying theme which unites Catholics, Protestants, and Jews," declared the Very Reverend Monsignor John J. Egan, speaking on The Responsibility of Church and Synagogue as Institutions in the Community. "It cannot be rejected without at the same time rejecting our place in the community of the Judaeo-Christian faithful." "In one sense, it may matter little what happens to minority groups in America," said President Benjamin E. Mays of Morehouse College, the conference chairman. "But it matters much what happens to the soul of America, to our democracy, and to our Judeo-Christian faith."[20]

Not that the conference was all sweetness and light. Black delegates, who constituted a quarter of those in attendance, criticized the overwhelmingly white composition of the steering committee and complained that the only blacks featured on the program were Chairman Mays himself and Martin Luther King, Jr. But the whites were quick with their mea culpas, and the protest turned into a set piece perfectly in line with the conference's basic scenario of repentance and reform. Discord of a less seemly kind, however, was provoked by a young white Episcopalian lawyer named William Stringfellow. As first discussant of Abraham Heschel's plenary address, Stringfellow, who lived and worked among the poor of Harlem, insisted that the most the conference ("too little, too late, and too lily white") could achieve was to weep for the failure of the churches on the race issue. The only *real* issue, he claimed, was "baptism" (by which he seemed to mean the unity of all men in Christ); and he declared that an invitation to address the delegates ought to have been extended to New York's charismatic Black Muslim leader Malcolm X.

If the "baptism" remark offended the Jews and embarrassed the Christians, the mention of Malcolm waved a red flag in front of the whole assemblage. For by 1963 the anti-white, anti-integrationist, anti-Christian Nation of Islam had assumed a typological significance in American liberal culture. "Their doctrine is hair-raising . . . in every way the exact counterpart of the White Supremacy lie, and as carefully buttressed with pseudo-religious and historically distorted myths," wrote the Congregationalist church bureaucrat Robert W. Spike in a review of Eric Lincoln's 1961 volume *The Black Muslims in America.* Yet, Spike acknowledged, the Muslims were thriving just because of the lack of progress in civil rights since the 1954 Supreme Court desegregation decision. "It is in this light that the passive resistance movement, the leadership of Martin Luther King and the sit-ins have to be understood. If only the opponents of these movements could see how magnificently restrained these are in contrast to what is altogether possible in the Muslim threat!"[21] Martin or Malcolm, that was the choice. It was not a cautionary tale told only by white liberals.

James Baldwin, quintessentially the Angry Negro Writer of the time, began his 1962 *New Yorker* piece "Letter from a Region of My Mind" by describing his own spiritual odyssey from teenaged preacher prodigy to apostate from a church that was too exclusive, that had rejected his Jewish schoolmates, that did not practice the love it preached. Then came the Muslims: "In the hall, as I was waiting for the elevator, someone shook my hand and said, 'Goodbye, Mr. James Baldwin. We'll soon be addressing you as Mr. James X.' And I thought, for an awful moment, My God, if this goes on much longer, you probably will." So Mr. Baldwin pays a visit to the Chicago home of the Black Muslim leader the Honorable Elijah Muhammad and finds himself powerfully affected by the man and his disciples.

He will not, "in order to pacify the white liberal conscience," dissent from Elijah's grim view of the situation of blacks in America: "Things are as bad as the Muslims say they are."[22]

In the end, though, Baldwin presented his *New Yorker* readers with the most Christian of messages: "I am very much concerned that American Negroes achieve their freedom here in the United States. But I am also concerned for their dignity, for the health of their souls, and must oppose any attempt that Negroes may make to do to others what has been done to them." Elijah, for all his justifiable rage, remains a type of evil. And as for "the white man," his only release is "to become black himself, to become a part of that suffering and dancing country that he now watches wistfully from the heights of his lonely power." So the Negro becomes Isaiah's suffering servant, an agent of salvation by way of imitation, of *imitatio Christi*. Refusal to pacify the white liberal conscience did not mean rejecting what it stood for. To Baldwin, the Nation of Islam represented an extreme embodiment of the twisted, fanatical church of his youth; Elijah reminded him of his own devout, embittered father. The "Letter" (reprinted as "Down at the Cross" in *The Fire Next Time*) only strengthened the case for an activist, nonexclusive, adhesional faith.[23]

Thus, let the radical Stringfellow rumble as he would, a place did not have to be made for Malcolm X at the National Conference on Religion and Race; the followers of Elijah Muhammad were beyond the Judeo-Christian pale. And for the better part of a year, at least, the ecumenical ministry held the field, achieving its most memorable triumph in the nation's capital the following August. It is worth recalling that the success of the historic March on Washington was anything but assured. Civil rights legislation was pending in Congress, and the anything but prophetically inclined Kennedy administration sought to prevent a massive street demonstration that might only harden the opposition. George Meany's AFL-CIO (though not Walter Reuther's UAW) refused its backing. But the churches were there, institutionally and in force; ministers, priests, and rabbis linked arms to be counted. The high point, of course, was Martin Luther King's brilliant address from the Lincoln Memorial, which threw patriotic and Biblical language together according to the highest traditions of American rhetoric. King's vision of a racially harmonious nation, proceeding from state to Southern state ("I have a dream that one day on the red hills of Georgia . . . that one day, even the state of Mississippi . . . that one day, down in Alabama . . ."), culminated in the messianic words of Deutero-Isaiah: "I have a dream that one day every valley shall be exalted, every hill and mountain shall be made low . . . and the glory of the Lord will be revealed and all flesh shall see it together." Then came the first stanza of "America," and finally, a summons for freedom to ring across the land so that "all of God's children—black men and white men, Jews and Gentiles, Catholics and Protestants" would be able to sing, in the words of the old Negro spiritual, "Free at last, free at last; thank God Almighty, we are free at last."

The following year (in a book whose title, My People Is the Enemy, was antithetical to King's redemptive appeal), William Stringfellow contended that the churches ought not boast about having recruited most of the fifty thousand white marchers on Washington; it had become clear by the summer of 1963, he said, that "the Negro revolution . . . would prevail." Thus: "Even in this burst of direct involvement in the demonstrations . . . they are again followers of public policy, neither leaders in social change nor prophets in the land." Such contempt for those lacking prophetic priority—an attitude that would become common later in the decade—missed the point, which was more nearly grasped by James Reston when he wrote, "The first significant test of the Negro march on Washington will come in the churches and synagogues of the country this weekend. . . . as moral principles preceded and inspired political principles in this country, as the church preceded the Congress, so there will have to be a moral revulsion to the humiliation of the Negro before there can be significant political relief." Whether the handwriting was on the wall or not, the Negro revolution required a consensus of support in the wider society, and that meant white religious involvement. Even with the success of the march, it took the death of one

president and the full commitment of his more legislatively
adroit successor to get a civil rights bill worthy of the name
through the Congress of the United States.[24]

If King's speech at the Lincoln Memorial was a vision of
the godly kingdom according to Isaiah, his other great civil
rights text was in the prophetic tradition of Amos denouncing
the priests of Israel for truckling to power. This was the "Letter
from Birmingham Jail," composed back in April in response to
a public statement from eight Alabama clergymen (Protestant,
Catholic, and Jewish) which criticized his latest campaign
against segregation as "unwise and untimely." King pictured
himself in the middle of the road, between the apathetic of his
race and the Black Muslims; and after detailing his reasons for
being in Birmingham, he declared his unhappiness with the
white churches—with the contemporary church as "archde-
fender of the status quo." What was needed was moral leadership in the manner of the Hebrew prophets, of Saint Paul, of
Martin Luther: the South would one day know that those who
had demonstrated at lunch counters "were in reality standing
up for what is best in the American dream and for the most
sacred values in our Judaeo-Christian heritage." "I hope this
letter finds you strong in the faith," King's final paragraph
irenically began—but also ironically, for how could they,
given what he had earlier said, be strong in the faith? "If today's church does not recapture the sacrificial spirit of the
early church, it will lose its authenticity, forfeit the loyalty of
millions, and be dismissed as an irrelevant social club with no
meaning for the twentieth century." Yet even should the
church fail, the civil rights struggle would triumph. "We will
win our freedom because the sacred heritage of our nation and
the eternal will of God are embodied in our echoing demands."
Shape up, in other words, or you will have separated your-
selves not only from the divine will but from the prophetic
mission of America itself.[25]

Were Birmingham's tri-faith clergymen (not to mention
their flocks) already separated from the faithful Judeo-Christians of America? King's hint recalled the summary judgment
rendered a few years earlier by the Louisiana novelist Walker

Percy. Percy, a Catholic intellectual more concerned with theological justice than with evangelical promise, had claimed that Southern society, for all its churchiness, was not really Christian, or at least that its upper-class leaders weren't. They were, rather, citizens of the ancient Stoic type, who until recently had looked after the Negroes as an act of noblesse oblige, and presided over a genteel community of manners based on their own self-esteem and the "extraordinary native courtesy and dignity" of the Negroes. But now, said Percy, that time was over; the Negro was demanding his rights, and the Southern gentleman, joining a White Citizens' Council or simply lapsing into silence, was happy to let him "taste the bitter fruits of his insolence." How different was the Christian scheme of things, where what the Stoic found intolerable simply became "the sacred right which must be accorded the individual, whether deemed insolent or not." Archbishop Rummel of New Orleans had declared segregation a sin (this was 1956); sooner or later Southerners would have to face up to their Christian heritage and answer him. "And the good pagan's answer is no longer good enough for the South."[26]

When Percy returned to the theme in 1965, some significant updating was required; in the wake of the collapse of "Stoic excellence," the Southern Negro had acquired a new ally. This was not, however, the upper-class Christian for whom Percy had hoped—Southern Christendom had still not faced up to "the single great burning issue in American life." The new ally was "the liberal humanist, who is more likely than not, frankly post-Christian in his beliefs." Midway through the decade, the white wing of the civil rights movement had ceased to be the preserve of the churches; as an example, Percy pointed to the Mississippi Summer Project of 1964, which, despite the sponsorship of the National Council of Churches, had drawn mostly nonreligious volunteers. If the South's professed Christians had stumbled, what, then, of these good pagans? They were, certainly, doing God's work. Yet Percy, the traditional-minded believer, was not prepared to say that the answer of "the Cambridge–Berkeley axis" was good enough for the South. There were other theologically inclined souls, though, who did not shrink from breaking down the wall that kept such representatives of "the victorious technological democratic society" outside the commonwealth of faith.[27]

Nineteen sixty-five, indeed, witnessed the biggest theological commotion to hit America since the Scopes trial of forty years before. On October 17, The New York Times published an article headed " 'New' Theologians See Christianity Without God." Hard on its heels came Ved Mehta's series of New Yorker pieces on "The New Theologian," which discovered much the same thing. This journalistic coincidence gave birth to a full-fledged media event, which achieved its apotheosis in red and black on Time's April 8, 1966, cover: IS GOD DEAD? Suddenly four junior theology professors unhappy with supernaturalist religion found themselves scandalizing clergy and laity across the country. Together, Thomas Altizer, William Hamilton, Paul Van Buren, and Gabriel Vahanian—who until then had barely been aware of one another's existence—became known as the "Death of God" theologians (though Van Buren would have nothing to do with the phrase and the others disagreed on what it meant). Much of the scandal lay in the fact that, unlike Friedrich Nietzsche, the first evangelist of God's demise, they insisted on retaining their Christian status.

As with the council then wrapping up its affairs in Rome (no small media event itself), the task at hand for the Death of God theologians was aggiornamento. But where Vatican II devoted itself to updating the religious medium (ecclesiastical practice and relations with those outside the Church), they focused on the message. Theirs was a grand renunciation of the neo-orthodox leap of faith grounded in the thought of the great neo-orthodox of the previous generation; above all they embraced neo-orthodoxy's critique of man-made "religion." The seminaries had recently been seized by a passion for Dietrich Bonhoeffer, the young German theologian executed by the Nazis for plotting against Hitler. Bonhoeffer, whose last, scattered writings postulated a "religionless Christianity," had struggled with the problem of bearing Christian witness in a secular age—how to "speak in a secular way of God." America's theological vanguard went further, asking how, in a secular age, to create a Godless Christianity.

To what end? Looking back from the far side of the decade, Garry Wills called Death of God theology "religion's way of crying from the tomb; a confession of lost energies" designed to channel "the secular world's unquestionable liveliness . . . toward our moribund religion."[28] But whose moribund religion? That the technical writings of a handful of young theologians could create such consternation would seem to suggest that religion was in fact alive and kicking. To be sure, those writings, taken up as they were with ongoing matters of academic theology, did not concern themselves with how religion actually functioned in the outside world. But a more worldly spiritual politics could be detected in their preoccupation with adapting faith to the present human condition—a condition assumed (without discussion) to be implacably secular. The politics was made explicit in a 1965 religious best-seller which became, in its way, the Death of God counterstroke to Herberg's neo-orthodox *Protestant Catholic Jew*: Harvey Cox's *The Secular City*.

Cox, then a young assistant professor of Theology and Culture at the Andover Newton Theological School, ebulliently announced the good news that secularization, far from being the enemy of religion, actually represented "an authentic consequence of biblical faith." Christians should therefore "support and nourish" a process that disenchanted nature, desacralized politics, and deconsecrated values. Growing up in rural Pennsylvania had immunized him to Protestant nostalgia for small-town churchly community; his book celebrated "technopolis," where the living was free and mobile, and the style pragmatic and profane. To be "where the action is," as he put it, the Church needed to behave accordingly—coolly promoting social progress while exorcising prejudice and hidebound, unsecular thinking. And if he stopped short of proclaiming the death of God, Cox did declare a moratorium on "God talk." For since, in the secular city, "the political is replacing the metaphysical as the characteristic mode of grasping reality," it was only right for religious folk to drop theology and pick up urbanology.[29]

Written in the warm afterglow of the Kennedy administration, The Secular City offered up a New Frontiersman's gospel; the martyred president appeared in its pages as an avatar of the pragmatic urban reformer. Whether JFK would, in his cool, pragmatic way, have spent five days in a Southern, jail for "taking part in a civil rights demonstration" (as the back cover proclaimed the author to have done), the book forbore to say. Yet no more than the Death of God theologians did Cox intend to fold up the tabernacle and steal away into the secular night. He not only expected the Church to be "God's Avant-Garde"; with the clever paradox of the secular-as-religious, he did away in an instant with Percy's troublesome post-Christians. The victorious technological democratic society was simply the latest product of the factory of faith. The Church, the New Frontier, the Cambridge–Berkeley axis—all were gathered under the Coxian umbrella, where there was neither secular nor sacred, just one great and good adhesional enterprise. But already, in 1965, the cities were burning. And it would soon turn out that when it came to grasping reality in the 1960s, the metaphysical mode was not so uncharacteristic after all.

7 ■ ***B*REAKING THROUGH**

I N the late summer of 1969, Americans had their attention directed for nearly a week to the Judean wilderness. Early on the morning of September 2, a young woman had stumbled into an Arab work camp near the Dead Sea after clambering all night through some of the most inhospitable territory on earth. She and her husband, it seemed, had set out from Jerusalem the previous day in a rented Ford Cortina, intending to take a back road to the site of the ancient holy community at Qumram, where the Dead Sea Scrolls had been discovered. Somehow, they had gotten lost, driven as far as the car would go, then set out on foot. When the man could walk no farther, his wife had proceeded in search of help. The man was the resigned Episcopal bishop of California, James Albert Pike. An intensive search was immediately mounted for "the controversial 56-year-old churchman," as the *New York Times* correspondent put it.

Controversial. The adjective clung to Pike as if it were a divine attribute. In the country's most genteel denomination, he was a notorious enthusiast for liberal causes. For the better part of the decade, he had been the object of one or another heresy charge before his House of Bishops. Since 1966, he had proselytized for parapsychology and spiritualism. In December of 1968, he had been married—for the third time and against ecclesiastical wishes—to a former student. A few months later, he had taken to the pages of *Look* to announce that he and his wife had decided to abandon the Church in favor of an organization he called The Foundation for Religious Transition.

What had he been up to, venturing in 120-degree heat through the cave-studded desert where, according to Matthew and Luke, Satan had tempted Jesus with all the kingdoms of the world? In a book published the following year, Mrs. Pike told of his conviction that this, his sixth trip to the Holy Land, would bring about "the big breakthrough—spiritually." On the night of September 6, in her hotel room, she saw a vision of Death as a kindly woman, of Jim's body in a reclining position, of Jim's spirit leaving the body and ascending in a long white column to the top of a canyon, there to be welcomed by a cloudlike crowd of people from the other side, including Paul Tillich and Robert Kennedy. The following day, Pike's body was finally found, in something like the posture she had envisioned, putrefying on a rocky ledge near the bottom of a deep wadi. He had come upon pools of fresh water, but had gone on, apparently until he slipped and fell. "I have no doubt," wrote Diane Kennedy Pike, "that that breakthrough came for Jim during his hours alone in the desert."

Some years later, in a short, eviscerating essay, Joan Didion called Jim Pike "a Michelin to his time and place." He was, at the least, a paradigm of postwar spiritual politics, from his adhesional awakening, through a heyday in reform, and on to the final bursting apart. "Oh yes! Oh yes!" he exclaimed to William Stringfellow, as the reporters and TV cameras gathered round at the trial of the Catonsville Nine. "This is where it's at! This is where the action is!" When it came to the religious action, no one had a nose like Bishop Pike.[1]

Born in Oklahoma, raised in Southern California as a Roman Catholic, he had begun a promising professional life as a lawyer in Washington during the war when he joined the

Episcopal Church and decided to make a career of it. He was ordained in 1946, just in time for the postwar revival, and by 1949 was ensconced as chaplain of Columbia University with a mandate from its new president, Dwight D. Eisenhower, to turn the religion department into a going concern. Within a couple of years students were flocking to attend an array of new courses, some taught by Reinhold Niebuhr and some by Paul Tillich; and soon the chaplain had moved on to the deanship of the Cathedral of St. John the Divine, where he started packing them in with his jazzy, slightly irreverent sermons. Pastoral and apologetic books began issuing from his pen; his contribution to the religious self-help literature of the day, dictated overnight, boxed the spiritual compass by drawing its title from, of all things, a line of Kierkegaard's: "What is Anxiety? It is *The Next Day*." For those who didn't choose to read, there was always "The Dean Pike Show," Episcopalianism's answer to Fulton Sheen, which aired Sunday mornings for six years on ABC.

He returned to California in episcopal triumph in 1958, though his election by the House of Bishops had been a close thing. He had a reputation as a publicity hound; he had spoken out against McCarthyism and censorship and in favor of birth control; he had gained the lasting enmity of a number of Southern bishops for having publicized (and thereby forced the reversal of) the segregation policy of the denomination's seminary at the University of the South in Sewanee, Tennessee. Yet if Pike was a liberal, he was the churchiest of the breed. He adored High Anglicanism's pomp and circumstance, and in New York had made sure that his subordinates were always attired in what he determined to be authentic garb. His was an anglophiliac vision of Church as Establishment, and if that meant pastoral outreach it also meant tweaking Cardinal Spellman's nose by registering St. John the Divine with the State as "The Cathedral of New York." In San Francisco, he spared no effort to raise the millions required to complete Grace Cathedral, his Gothic pile on Nob Hill. That he put up stained-glass portraits of such secular luminaries as Albert Einstein, Thurgood Marshall, and John Glenn merely attested to his exalted view of the Church as inclusive moral superintendent of the entire culture. When Eugene Carson Blake, head of the National Council of Churches, decided to announce a grand scheme for ecumenical church union, he did it, during the council's 1960 general assembly, from the pulpit of Grace Cathedral. "I knew," he later commented, "that being where Pike was bishop, the sermon would be heard."[2] The plan became known as the Blake-Pike Proposal.

Good establishmentarian that he was, Pike assumed a "broad church" approach to theology: the Episcopalian establishment was to be open to as many views as possible. Thus, when the House of Bishops, meeting in 1960, issued a pastoral letter declaring the church "irrevocably committed to the historic creeds," he commented that should the letter be formally promulgated, he himself could be found heretical. Soon after, when his contribution to The Christian Century's 1960 How My Mind Has Changed series hinted at doubts about the Trinity, the Virgin Birth, and Salvation Through Christ Alone, some decided to take him at his word, and the first of the heresy complaints was lodged against him. What began as a latitudinarian (if characteristically provocative) doctrinal stance was before long swept up in the unexpected hoopla over radical theology. Never one to turn back when he found himself on the crest of a wave, Pike flaunted his friendship with John Robinson, the Anglican bishop whose best-selling assault on traditional theism, Honest to God, in 1963 provoked a British forerunner of the American Death of God controversy. "The fact is we are in the midst of a theological revolution," preached Pike before a standing-room-only crowd at the 1964 Episcopal General Convention. The Trinity, he declared (doubts having hardened into fixed opinions), was an "irrelevancy." Sure, the Death of God theologians would in due course pooh-pooh Pike's views as—by the theological standards of the academy—derivative, unexceptionable, even conservative. Sure, the House of Bishops would ultimately (in 1967) tiptoe away from trying him for heresy. James Pike nevertheless appeared in the public arena as a leading radical. Broad church had become avant-garde.

And as in theology, so in politics. At the same General Convention, Pike directly attacked the Southern bishops for being soft on racism; and he gained a lifelong friend (and two-time biographer) in the impetuous William Stringfellow when he signed a "statement" of Stringfellow's condemning the current Republican presidential ticket for "transparent exploitation of racism among white citizens."[3] Pike's presence the following year at the march from Selma to Birmingham, Alabama—the last hurrah of civil rights ecumenism—may have been tolerable to the more conservative members of his California flock; but his support for the new economic agenda of Martin Luther King, and his backing of Caesar Chavez' efforts to organize the migrant farm workers of the state, were something else again. By the time he resigned his bishopric in 1966, the man who had sought to make Episcopal cathedrals central to American urban life had little good to say about what he now liked to call "the standard-brand churches."

The final phase began with the suicide of his son, James Junior, in February of 1966. It was after that that the bishop turned in his diocese for a fellowship at Robert Hutchins' Center for the Study of Democratic Institutions; after that that, like many bereaved before him, he succumbed to the designs of mediums claiming to put him in touch with the lost loved one. He spent much of the following year barnstorming the country, laying his doctrinal views before the public preparatory to a final showdown in the House of Bishops; but when he was more or less vindicated, the news was drowned out by a new commotion resulting from his participation in a televised seance. Personal tragedy became public witness: *The Other Side*, an apologia for spiritualism written in collaboration with Diane, appeared in 1968. By then his long-time mistress had killed herself, a daughter had attempted to do the same, and his second marriage was over and done with. But Pike pressed on. Knowing next to nothing about how Fathers Daniel and Philip Berrigan and seven others had poured blood on files of the Catonsville, Maryland, draft board, he got himself to the trial, assumed the office of assistant defense counsel, and brought a gathering of hundreds of supporters to their feet with an oration declaring his own conversion to the antiwar cause.

Yet the consuming passion of Pike's last years was not theological *aggiornamento* or spiritualism or protesting his government's policy in Vietnam. Rather, The Foundation for Religious Transition, in the persons of himself and Diane, was taken up with what looked to be a most academic study of Christian origins. After his death, Diane and her brother Scott (who had helped in the search for the bishop's body) devoted themselves to putting together the account of a new search for the historical Jesus that James Pike had not lived to write— featuring at the head of each chapter a lengthy quotation, as if from the other side, from Pike himself. With its hundred pages of notes and ten of scholarly bibliography, *The Wilderness Revolt* is more than an historical romance; but it makes no secret of its desire to portray a Jesus "relevant" to the present. The Jesus who emerges from its pages is Jesus the apocalyptic nationalist, linked in his expectation of an imminent end of times to the Zealots who chose to perish in the Judean mountain retreat of Masada rather than succumb to the Roman legions. All roads somehow seemed to lead to first-century Judea: where, before the creeds were hammered out, there was room for theological maneuver; where, before the age of science, psychic phenomena were accepted as a normal part of life; where, before the Church was built up and allied to the state, opposition to an imperial government was the rule; where, in the life and times of Christianity's God and founder, the action eternally was.

In the end, the very model of a postwar establishmentarian attached himself to, *converted to*, the profoundly antiestablishment faith of a charismatic leader. The faith was at once mystical and political, and why not? Just as earlier, in *The Next Day*, Pike had looked for an audience of positive-thinking Pealites and neo-orthodox Kierkegaardians, so this Jesus of his —part guru, part revolutionary—could appeal to both hemispheres of the contemporary counterculture: the communards of the New Age and the zealots of the New Left. In death as in life, Pike reached for the *tour de force*. Not that this last *tour de force* was meant to appeal to the ordinary Episcopalian-in-the-pew; Pike's Jesus accorded ill with standard-brand piety. But the Bishop of California had hardly claimed to be sacrific-

ing all to follow his Lord; the ship he left seemed to him to be
sinking. When Grace Cathedral lost its controversial master in
1966, Watts was in ashes and Haight-Ashbury in full flower.
The game was up for the grand adhesional mode that had
served James Pike in such good stead.

Even its emblem, the Judeo-Christian tradition, was falling
on hard times. As powerful as the concept had been in the
great days of the civil rights movement, after mid-decade it
began to strike commentators as an historical artifact. How
could such a thing have established itself in the public mind?
In 1966, Robert Gordis offered his impressions: the growth of
an interfaith movement after World War I, fear of Communism
(!) during the Depression, the rise of a pluralist ethic after
World War II.[4] For Rabbi Gordis, this was not just the history
of an illusion. For others it was that and worse.

In 1970, the novelist and lay theologian Arthur A. Cohen
brought out a collection of his essays under the title *The Myth
of the Judeo-Christian Tradition*. In freshly written introduc-
tory and concluding sections, Cohen argued that the roots of
the myth lay in the eighteenth-century Enlightenment, which,
hostile to all revealed religion, had conceived Judaism and
Christianity as partakers of a common untruth. As for the defi-
nition of the Judeo-Christian tradition "as such," he attributed
that to the nineteenth-century German Protestant scholars engaged in the Higher Criticism of the Bible; their aim had been
to acknowledge the Jewish dimension of Christianity while
cutting away those aspects of Judaism antipathetic to their
"pure, virtuous Kantian" Protestantism. The result was a "de-
Judaizing of Christian theology."[5] Even if true, this account
would have been a red herring; Kantian Protestantism was the
chosen adversary of the Protestant "Hebraism" which had animated theological usage of the phrase in the present day—
when, as Cohen allowed, "the Judeo-Christian tradition" had
"come to full expression." His object, though, was to implicate
exponents of the tradition in the twentieth century's great
crime against the Jewish people; the de-Judaization of Christian theology, he asserted, was responsible for "the pitiful in-
ability of the Protestant (and to a slightly—but only slightly—

lesser extent, Catholic) Church to oppose German National Socialism." That, of course, was to turn the political history inside out, since it was just in order to combat Nazism that "the Judeo-Christian tradition" had first been pressed into service.

Cohen did gesture at the neo-orthodox sponsorship of the idea, saying that it had thrived on a Christian desire "to affirm a renewed connection with the Hebrew Bible" and a Jewish desire to join with Christianity in the battle against secularism. But this he waved away as a "swarm of fideist passion" which omitted "the sinew and bone of actuality"—the rift between those for whom the Messiah was yet to come and those for whom He had come already. It was a rift so wide that even those "compatible truths" shared by Judaism and Christianity were insufficient grounds to suggest "the presence of something more, a *tertium quid* to which both communities appeal and to which both seem more respondent than to their historical enmity." That didn't mean war: the book concluded with hopes for a "Judeo-Christian humanism" through which anger could be set aside and the common task embraced of working for a better world. But neo-orthodoxy's renunciation of exclusivist theology, its adhesional groping toward theological common ground, was categorically rejected; if each religion were to remain true to itself, antagonism had to be preserved. "The only authentic Judeo-Christian tradition is that God bears both communities down to the end of time unreconciled."[6]

Commentary, the organ of the American Jewish Committee, gave its blessing to *The Myth of the Judeo-Christian Tradition* by printing excerpts prior to publication. In the Jewish monthly *Midstream*, the liberal Talmudic scholar Jacob Neusner celebrated Cohen as, among American-born writers, "the most brilliant contemporary theologian of Judaism without qualification or exception." *Commonweal's* reviewer applauded the assault on a concept that was "the catch-all of textbook writers, Western Civ. lectures, Brotherhood Week toastmasters, and Jews and Christians who cannot think of anything else to speak of to one another when it comes to religious convictions." And so it went. True, Father Oesterreicher, whose Judeo-Christian Institute was flayed in one chapter, attacked the author both for his polemical style and for what he had to say: "I thus beg to dissent from the eulogists of Mr. Cohen's book." Yet his was the voice of another day; the Judeo-Christian tradition had lost its charm.[7]

Why? For America's Jews, at any rate, one event was critical: the Six-Day War of June 3–8, 1967. In the weeks and days before the war—as Egypt massed its troops, secured the withdrawal of the United Nations peacekeeping force, and barred Israeli passage into the Gulf of Aqaba—they began to have visions of a second Jewish holocaust. Suddenly the financial contributions were coming in faster than could be tabulated, and in cash instead of the usual pledges; between the beginning of the crisis and the end of the war the United Jewish Appeal alone received $100 million. The money came not only from the usual sources but also from those who had never given, whose Jewishness, indeed, seemed marginal at best: secular-minded academics, Unitarians of Jewish background, the assimilated of the assimilated. Rebellious youth? Seventy-five hundred young people volunteered to go to Israel to help with the civilian work. But this high volume of concern found very little echo in the Christian community—an ad here, a statement of support there, signed by a few individuals at the beseeching of Jewish leaders. And from the official organs and institutions of Christendom, ambivalence or silence. Two weeks after the complete victory that seemed, to Israelis themselves, little short of miraculous, Jewish grievance at the churches broke into public view. At a rabbinical assembly in Los Angeles, Balfour Brickner, as Reform Judaism's head of interfaith activities, attacked the "Christian establishment" for its apparent inability to "take a strong stand on what it considered to be a political issue." A few days later, the president of the Orthodox Rabbinical Council of America, Pesach Z. Levovitz, expressed his "deep disappointment" over the failure of "major segments of the world and American Christian community to raise their voices in defense of Israel when before the outbreak of hostilities President Nasser of Egypt was threatening the annihilation of its more than two million Jews." Interfaith discussion should cease, said Levowitz, until

Christian leaders made clear their support for Israel's territorial and political integrity.[8]

Encountering these remarks in *The New York Times*, the aging Henry P. Van Dusen fired off a letter to the editor which read, in part: "All persons who seek to view the Middle East problem with honesty and objectivity stand aghast at Israel's onslaught, the most violent, ruthless (and successful) aggression since Hitler's blitzkrieg across Western Europe in the summer of 1940, aiming not at victory but at annihilation— the very objective proclaimed by Nasser and his allies which had drawn support to Israel." Blitzkrieg, annihilation—the comparison was, to say no more, inflammatory, but the Christian establishments, Protestant and Catholic, did not hurry to dissociate themselves from the former president of Union Theological Seminary. They had been ambivalent about the State of Israel from its creation, and they now resented what they felt to be unwarranted Jewish demands. Monsignor George G. Higgins, secretary to the Commission for Catholic–Jewish Relations of the Bishops' Committee for Ecumenical and Interreligious Affairs, charged that the rabbis' "criticism of the Catholic Church in the United States, whether they realize it or not, is a form of ecumenical or interreligious blackmail." *The Christian Century*, describing itself as "appalled," asserted that Christians "will not sign a blank check."[9]

In its own eyes, the National Council of Churches struggled for neutrality. On the eve of the war, its General Board had managed to adopt a resolution supporting the UN's peacekeeping functions. On July 7, a new resolution urged international "acceptance" of the State of Israel at the same time as it criticized Israel's "territorial expansion by armed force" and "unilateral retention of occupied lands." And then there was the distress which ensued when, at a Rally for Israel in Washington on June 3, news of the cease-fire cut short the remarks of the NCC executive secretary, R. H. Edwin Espy. Lest his presence be construed as NCC partisanship for the Jewish state, the *Century* published his undelivered disclaimer: "Our identification is not of course exclusively with any one community, one belligerent, or one set of national aspirations. . . .

Had we been invited to attend a corresponding meeting of the Arab community in the United States we would have been bound by our principles to bring the identical message—the plea for peace with justice and freedom which we derive from our Judeo-Christian heritage." Such use of Judeo-Christian rhetoric to avow evenhandedness between the Jews and their enemies was a far cry from the days when the enemies were the Nazis.[10]

The year before, in the journal *Judaism*, the Orthodox rabbi and theologian Eliezer Berkovitz had reviewed the history of Jewish–Christian relations in the course of an attack on Jewish–Christian theological dialogue. ("What is usually referred to as the Judeo-Christian tradition exists only in Christian or secularist fantasy. As far as Jews are concerned, Judaism is fully sufficient. There is nothing in Christianity for them.") In the following issue, a combative Rabbi Neusner compared the article to the sermon of a Black Muslim preacher: "a public display of private hostilities and fantasies." Hardly was the Six-Day War over, however, when Neusner repented himself of what he had said: the behavior of the American churches, he admitted to *Judaism's* readers, had proved Berkovitz right. "Much has changed for me, and, I believe, for others as well." If the war taught any lesson in theology, it was that Judaism was not just that version of the common faith that went without Jesus. In the words of Willard G. Oxtoby, a Presbyterian minister and Yale professor who was no supporter of Israel, "To discover the heart of Judaism we must shift the focus from the messiahship of Jesus to the peoplehood of Israel." The point was made again and again by Jewish writers, and for them also it ranked as a discovery; for the depth of the American Jewish response had been wholly unexpected. The Jewish people of America had always given their support to Israel, but they had not emigrated there in large numbers, and had seemed content to adapt comfortably into their American Zion. In the crisis of 1967, they turned toward Jerusalem as never before.[11]

Nor was America about to say them nay. As the country found itself being sucked steadily into the morass of Vietnam, there was no lack of admiration for a nation capable of vanquishing its foes in the time God had taken to create the world. A day after the Israeli victory, the Honorable L. Mendel Rivers, Democrat of South Carolina and chairman of the House Armed Services Committee, stood near the lunch counter in the Democratic cloakroom and declaimed. "Now, I don't want to hear anyone say anything against my Jews. Why, I'd trade a hundred F-111s for one Moshe Dayan." Rivers was known for his philo-Semitism (he liked to boast about the three synagogues in his Charleston district), but he was preaching to the converted. Thanks to the efforts of an enterprising lobbyist, members of Congress of all political and religious persuasions could be seen on the House floor sporting Dayan-like eye patches. In an Associated Press survey published on June 16, 364 out of the 438 senators and representatives agreed that Israel should not withdraw its troops without assurances of national security and the right to use disputed waterways. As Washington went, so went the nation: a Gallup Poll, released on June 11, showed sympathy for Israel running at 55 percent, compared with 4 percent for the Arabs. And attitudes did not shift in the following months and years; until the oil shortage and Anwar Sadat unsettled the equation, the Middle East featured the United States and Israel (perhaps with Iran and Turkey thrown in) versus the Russians and the Arabs.

In 1973, Nathan Rotenstreich, professor of philosophy and former rector of the Hebrew University in Jerusalem, wrote that the American notion of a "Judaeo-Christian civilization" was simply a "device" to make gentiles believe that they shared a common tradition with the Jews, and to convince Jews that they partook not only of the universal secular culture but of the universal Christian one as well. "There seems to be a kind of suspicion, vis-à-vis the Jews, that they have to be convinced of the identity between themselves and the surrounding world, lest they cultivate their own distinctiveness."[12] But in the aftermath of 1967, American Jews discovered that an intense identification with the Jewish state did not evoke the charge of divided loyalty, that the cultivation of ethnic distinctiveness in no way detracted from acceptance in American society at large. (Indeed, the society was soon experiencing an enthusiasm for ethnic particularism, or "roots," of every kind.) Who needed the Judeo-Christian tradition?

"The glory of the Washington and Selma-to-Montgomery marches is that men and women converged upon those places out of a deep internal commitment," wrote David Polish, a rabbi from Evanston, Illinois, in *The Christian Century* in late July of 1967. "Jews should take pride in the knowledge that they were in the vanguard of those marches. They expected nothing in return . . . Yet we cannot but wonder why, when Israel the State and Israel the People stood with their backs to the Mediterranean, the same intense response of spirit and compassion was not forthcoming." Should the Christian clergy really have been expected to respond to the Mideast crisis the way they had to racism in the South? Within the Jewish community itself, opinion was divided. It was clear, though, that the politics of ecumenical witness had become far touchier, and for reasons that went far beyond the tension between church and synagogue provoked by the Six-Day War.[13]

The reasons related to the war in Vietnam. In its "Christians will not sign a blank check" editorial, *The Christian Century* had taken to task, though not by name, those few but prominent "Christian leaders" (Reinhold Niebuhr and Martin Luther King, Jr., among them) who, having opposed U.S. military involvement in Southeast Asia, then proceeded to "insist that the power of the United States be unleashed in the Middle East on the side of Israel." This "ideological flipflop," said the journal, had done its "greatest harm" to the peace movement in the United States, and in particular to an organization called Clergy and Laymen Concerned About Vietnam, to which "many of the switch-and-fight people," as well as a number of the *Century*'s own staff, belonged.[14]

Clergy and Laymen Concerned (at first just Clergy Concerned, and ultimately, Clergy and *Laity*) had come into being in November of 1965, when Roger LaPorte, one of Dorothy Day's young Catholic Workers, immolated himself on the steps of the United Nations as an act of antiwar protest. The group's founding fathers, in classic Protestant-Catholic-Jew array, were a young Lutheran pastor from Brooklyn named Richard Neuhaus, the Jesuit Daniel Berrigan, and Rabbi Abraham Heschel; when, after making their concern public at the United Nations church center, they were asked by Homer Bigart of *The New York Times* what they planned to do next, Heschel replied— to his colleagues' surprise—that they intended to organize the churches and synagogues of the country against the war. The largest sustaining peace group of its time was off and running.

The spiritual moment is best preserved in Robert Bellah's famous article "Civil Religion in America," which appeared in the journal *Daedalus* the following year. Bellah, a California sociologist whose field of expertise was religion in Tokugawa Japan, undertook to set straight the cultured despisers of "the American Shinto," "religion in general," and "the religion of the American Way of Life"; all such gibes, he felt, actually pointed to an American civil religion that was both authentically religious and *a good thing*. He carried no brief, of course, for "the American-Legion type of ideology that fuses God, country, and flag . . . to attack nonconformist and liberal ideas and groups of all kinds." What he had in mind was religious and religiously derived commitments to, for example, God and a higher law, or to covenant and sacrifice. He claimed that throughout the nation's history an evolving set of these commitments, institutionalized in ritual and articulated by presidents, had "served as a genuine vehicle of national religious self-understanding"; this had happened above all during two "times of trial," from which the civil religion had emerged as from a refiner's fire. The Revolutionary and Civil War periods had reckoned with the great issues, respectively, of independence and slavery. Now we were faced with a third such issue, "responsible action in a revolutionary world"; and the war was Vietnam. Bellah was glad to find that, as once with the Mexican–American war, "prophetic voices" were not wanting to oppose this military adventure. And he was confident that the nation would, as in the earlier times of trial, discover new civil religious symbols—in fact, would this time discover that "world civil religion" which had been the "eschatological hope" of American civil religion from the beginning. "To deny such an outcome would be to deny the meaning of America itself."[15]

This was, we might say, the last gasp of postwar adhesional liberalism—a final invocation of high common cause between religion and the state. But the argument itself, at least as applied to the present trial, was seriously flawed. For while opposition to the war with Mexico, enshrined in Thoreau's essay on civil disobedience, may have created a tradition of antiwar protest in America, it did not animate the kind of civil religious symbolism suitable for public ritual and presidential articulation. Such symbolism arose not from the prophetic assault on bad wars, but from the priestly promotion of good ones. (The creation of the Judeo-Christian dogma during World War II is itself a case in point.) In order for the American civil religion to be refined or extended, the federal government must at some point join the crusade, and adopt the spiritual rhetoric as its own. Adhesion of this sort came about through the civil rights struggle, a "war" which the government eventually helped prosecute, and whose martyred hero, like the heroes of the Revolutionary and Civil wars, was in due course accorded his own national holiday. In the wake of Washington and Selma, there was briefly the hope that the enterprise could continue in the matter of Vietnam. But such was not to be.

On November 28, Clergy Concerned got its campaign off the ground with a teach-in–cum–rally in New York's Christ Church Methodist, at which four hundred clergymen manifested their support for the proposition "that the war in Vietnam is not a just one." Daniel Berrigan, however, was not there. Though told by his local Jesuit superior to keep his distance from the LaPorte affair, he had given a memorial talk comparing the suicide to the death of Christ, and was sent off to Latin America to cool his heels—convinced (wrongly, it happens) that this was at Cardinal Spellman's bidding. His place was marked by an empty chair on the platform beside Neuhaus and Heschel, and his brother, Philip, spoke in his stead. A number of other priests and nuns were in attendance too, but the hierarchy was conspicuous by its absence; not

until 1971—four years after Spellman's death and a year after
the invasion of Cambodia and the killings at Kent and Jackson
State—could the bishops bring themselves to break with the
American government on the war. Between their ingrained
anti-Communism and their long-standing support for the U.S.
military, the wonder is that they did so at all.[16]

Roman Catholic recusancy was only part of the problem.
Although Clergy and Laymen Concerned enjoyed the material
and moral support of the National Council of Churches, the
war in Vietnam stymied its constituent denominations in a
way civil rights had not. To raise the banner of Thoreau against
the government, to condemn unequivocally a war which many
of their members were waging, that they were not prepared to
do. "We were always fighting to get resolutions passed by the
churches," Neuhaus later recalled. And if his organization
helped make opposition to the war respectable, within a short
time respectable opposition didn't seem to amount to much.
By 1968 the real antiwar action was taking place unrespectably
on the campuses, in the streets, and underground. For all the
participation of churchfolk, it was not an ecumenical crusade.

In March, 1966, when he got back to New York, Daniel
Berrigan had gone to see Neuhaus. "You want to set up an
institution," he said. Neuhaus conceded that that was the idea.
"Well," said Dan, "that's not for me." The Berrigan style was
always to maintain the prophetic edge, to move on when acceptance threatened. "What a great feeling," he exclaimed
after a visit to Eastern Europe, "to be in a country where there's
no head of state going to church every Sunday and corrupting
it!" Once Clergy Concerned was on its way, it became for him
just "another liberal bag." The same went for the Catholic
Peace Fellowship, with its "softness and bureaucracy." And:
"Draft-card burning has become establishment . . . it's not the
time to burn draft cards anymore, but draft files!"

"Marching and protesting, as a viable or effective form of
protest, died shortly after Selma," declared one of the other
defendants at the Catonsville trial. "It has been institutionalized and legalized, and it is no longer effective." To be effective one had to be outside the system. Although Rabbi Heschel

and Pastor Neuhaus were there, and Bishop Pike and Harvey
Cox and Yale's William Sloane Coffin, and such secular luminaries of the antiwar movement as Rennie Davis and Benjamin
Spock, Catonsville was a Catholic affair—with Catholic defendants defying not only their government but their church as
well. When he took the stand, Daniel Berrigan did not hesitate
to strike back at his late imagined nemesis. "Cardinal Spellman . . . believed that the highest expression of faith for an
American Christian was to support military efforts. By his annual Christmas visits to troops across the world and specifically in Vietnam, he was placing an official seal of approval
upon our military adventures. And I had to say no to that, too.
I had to say 'no' to the Church . . . so much so that in the
autumn of 1965, by the conjunction of powers that remain
mysterious to me even now, I was exiled from the United
States to Latin America." Had he been exiled, interrupted an
alarmed Judge Thomsen, by the government? No, no, said Father Berrigan with a sly smile. The powers in question were
the cardinal and the Jesuit superiors. The most proximate
power was the archbishop of Baltimore, and he was quoted as
saying he "washed his hands" of the Catonsville Nine.
(Quipped Bishop Pike, "At least it shows he reads his Bible.")
Thus did the hierarchy, with the words of Pilate on its lips,
abandon to the government the prophets of the true church.[17]

But the word went forth. "I say that Jesus was, according
to the testimonies of the gospels, a criminal: not a mere nonconformist, not just a protester, more than a militant, not only
a dissident, not simply a dissenter, but a criminal. More than
that, as . . . Luke [23:1–2] . . . emphasizes, from the point of
view of the State and of the ecclesiastical authorities as well—
from the view of the establishment—Jesus was the most dangerous and reprehensible sort of criminal. He was found as one
'perverting [the] nation,' and 'forbidding . . . tribute' to the
State." This was William Stringfellow preaching on October
13, 1969, at a Cornell University service at which Daniel Berrigan, then waiting to appeal his Catonsville conviction, offi-
ciated. (A few months later, the appeal denied, he would be
arrested at Stringfellow's Block Island home as a fugitive from

justice by FBI agents posing as bird-watchers.) After the sermon, Stringfellow noted, "the students were delighted, the faculty bemused, the trustees, for the most part, enraged."[18] Here was religion on the antiestablishment barricades. Free the Jerusalem Thirteen!

Yet, as James Pike had recognized, antiestablishment religion was not just a matter of radical opposition to the war in Vietnam. Even the antiwar movement—or, as it simply called itself, the Movement—incorporated a radical spirituality which was in its own way as much of an assault on the prevailing religious order as antiwar "actions" were on the prevailing political one. In 1970, the United Church of Christ's Pilgrim Press published, and Knopf distributed, a volume which might (should a nuclear disaster wreak havoc on the historical record of the late twentieth century) serve future scholars as the Movement's own Dead Sea Scrolls. Assembled by a draft resister named Mitchell Goodman, *The Movement Toward a New America* is a compendium of texts, photographs, and drawings assembled from both the underground and the aboveground press, and grouped in sections like "The New Americans," "People of Color," "Rebellion Resistance Revolutionary Action," and "How to Live What to Do." Of its 750 pages, fewer than 30 are devoted to "What Price Salvation Now," but these ought to provide any postholocaust student of "Movement religion" with more than enough to chew on.

The heroes are the Berrigans, together with Father James Groppi and the Milwaukee Fourteen draft-file burners, and the Maryknoll nuns active in behalf of the oppressed of Latin America; all in all, nine of the twenty-three texts reflect one or another aspect of Catholic radicalism. Protestantism, by contrast, is acknowledged in only two texts: a leaflet headed "Seminarians Say: Church Is Full of Shit" and a 1970 column from the *Berkeley Tribe* commending the (post-Pike!) "establishment Episcopal Diocese of California" for supporting Berkeley's "radical Free Church." There is also a "wanted" poster for Jesus Christ ("wanted for sedition, criminal anarchy, vagrancy, and conspiracy to overthrow the established government"). But in addition to these manifestations of New Left

piety—leading off the entire section, in fact—was an article by
the mystical classicist Norman O. Brown asking for a return to
the "power of enthusiasm" which derived from Christian apo-
calypticism. Theodore Roszak, the man who coined the term
"counter culture," supplied his professorially distanced but
hardly unenthusiastic assessment of American youth in search
of "mythical-religious" consciousness: "a remarkable defection from the long-standing tradition of skeptical, secular in-
tellectuality that has served as the prime vehicle for 300 years
of scientific and technical development in the West." The poet
Allen Ginsberg, who, Roszak asserted, "claims a greater audience among dissenting youth than any Christian or Jewish
clergyman could hope to reach or stir," was represented by a
short statement urging return to the "Gnostic (formerly su-
pressed [sic] heretical) tradition in Western imagery." For a
"complete application of the above to U.S. POLITICS," Ginsberg
referred readers to his friend Gary Snyder's Earth House Hold;
and sure enough, the Beat-Buddhist poet's "Buddhism and the
Coming Revolution" can be found wrapping up the section.[19]

What were the Berrigans doing in a Norman O. Brown–
Gary Snyder sandwich? Six months before Catonsville, Philip
Berrigan and three associates (the Baltimore Four) had announced the first defacement of draft files by imploring their
fellow citizens "to judge our action against this nation's Judeo-
Christian tradition," but this was far too tame a rhetorical appeal by the West Coast standards of The Movement Toward a
New America. If the slogan of the day was Pogo's "We have
met the enemy and he is us," then "us" included the whole
mainstream spiritual enterprise. A sexual revolution was
under way, wrote a Seattle radical in 1966, which "promises
as its influence grows to give a shattering blow to rotten Judeo-
Christian morality with its sexual shame, guilt, and its person-
ality-destroying repressions." According to Gary Snyder, true
community would require support for cultural and economic
revolution, use of civil disobedience and voluntary poverty
and pacifism, affirmation of the right to take drugs and be
polygamous and homosexual: "worlds of behavior and custom
long banned by the Judaeo-Capitalist-Christian-Marxist West."

In the library of the Harvard Divinity School is the tape recording of a 1969 round table on the "new religious consciousness" chaired by James Pike and featuring Snyder, Ginsberg, and Harvey Cox. At one point, a voice from the audience asks Pike what the Christian religion is offering to the youth of today; after all, Zen and Tibetan Buddhist teaching are adapting to the psychedelic. Well, says Pike, he's seen reports, and if the data are right, Hinduism and Buddhism may be better for psychedelics than the Judeo-Christian faiths. Perhaps a Foundation for Religious Transition *was* the next order of business.[20]

For a guide to the transition, *The Movement Toward a New America* referred readers to a most curious ethnography published in 1968 by the University of California Press. Had it appeared a bit earlier, Carlos Castaneda's The Teachings of Don Juan would have served as a principal proof text for Roszak's 1969 best-seller The Making of a Counter Culture. (It did feature prominently in his follow-up volume of 1972, Where the Wasteland Ends.) The book recounts, in the first person, how a graduate student in anthropology at the University of California at Los Angeles goes off to the Southwest to research a thesis on medicinal herbs; meets a Yaqui Indian said to be very learned in peyote; and is accepted by the Indian, who turns out to be a sorcerer, as his apprentice. Instructed in the preparation and use of several hallucinogenic plants, the student encounters a realm of "non-ordinary reality" where, among other things, he experiences several theophanic visions of Mescalito, the personification of peyote. In the end, however, he terminates his quest to become "a man of knowledge" when it threatens to persuade him of the actual existence of this separate reality. Being the diligent doctoral candidate he is, the student cannot abandon his skeptical Western self. Did this or that apparently impossible thing really happen to me? You cannot think like that, he is told; such a question makes no sense. Near the conclusion of his four-year apprenticeship, he smokes a mushroom mixture and, becoming a crow, flies alongside three silvery birds. His master pronounces these birds the only thing of "great value" in the entire experience. "What was so special about them? They were just birds." "Not just birds—they were crows." "Were they white crows, don Juan? . . . Why did their feathers look silvery?" "Because you were seeing as a crow sees. A bird that looks dark to us looks white to a crow."[21]

William James, in a famous image, once likened the demonstration of spiritualism to overthrowing the law that all crows are black: "It is enough if you prove one single crow to be white." Now, it seemed, finding the white crow required not James's radical empiricism but an altered state of consciousness. Was the Yaqui sorcerer engaging in subtle repartee with the spirit of the Harvard professor? Not exactly, for Castaneda's enthnographic enterprise was in reality a fiction. General recognition of this, however, took some time. (In 1973, in fact, the UCLA anthropology department awarded Castaneda a Ph.D. for his third Don Juan volume, *Journey to Ixtlan*.) Meanwhile, the mythical don acquired millions of vicarious followers eager to keep up with his Boswell's breakthroughs behind the crust of the Western rationalist worldview.[22]

When don Juan displayed independent knowledge of what Carlos felt himself to be seeing and doing under the influence of drugs, the author called it "special consensus"—corroboration that the experiences of transcendence were in some sense real. As one looks over the array of religious movements in America between, say, 1965 and 1975, the impression is of an intense search for such special consensuses: the International Society for Krishna Consciousness, the Meher Baba Movement, Synanon, the Divine Light Mission of the Guru Maharaj Ji, the Church of Satan, the Children of God, the Unification Church, to name a few. Gurus were everywhere; communes, urban and rural, sprang up like mushrooms. How far did this conversional impulse affect the general population? For every devotee of Krishna consciousness, there remained thousands of Methodists and Baptists and Catholics going about their spiritual business in ways that had nothing to do with cults and communes. Yet in its radical turning toward new forms of belief and religious practice, the counterculture was symptomatic of a larger rejection of America's pre-Vietnam spirituality. Indeed, the era's most striking assault on the "general consensus" governing postwar religion came from a source diametrically opposed to the New Religious Consciousness.

At the same time that Castaneda was leading the way into the brave new world of psychedelic anthropology, another figure on the UCLA campus was busy adapting his calling to the Age of Aquarius. He was a staff member of the local Campus Crusade for Christ named Hal Lindsey, and in 1970 he worked his lectures and sermons up into a small volume called *The Late Great Planet Earth*. Though scarcely noticed even by the evangelical press, it became the best-selling book of the decade, with scores of printings ultimately flooding the United States with some 16 million copies. It was a tale of biblical prophecy told in the countercultural vernacular, and it went like this: Soon the Israelis will rebuild the Temple in Jerusalem and conclude a treaty with the dictator of the Revived Roman Empire, also known as the Antichrist. All saved Christians will then be seized into heaven ("The Rapture," or "Jesus' ultimate trip"), whereupon there will be a seven-year period of tribulation involving, first, the invasion of Israel by an Arab-African conspiracy headed by Egypt, followed by an invasion by the Russian confederacy. Russia and its allies will then be destroyed with Roman tactical nuclear weapons, and shortly thereafter the climactic battle of Armageddon will commence, between the forces of the empire and a 200-million-man Chinese army. Before humanity succeeds in destroying itself, Jesus will come to earth for the second time (along with His enraptured saints) and establish His one-thousand-year reign. Then, after a brief rebellion by Satan, the final judgment will occur. So the Bible says.

Known technically as dispensational premillennialism, this way of imagining the "end times" had been worked out and debated for a century in fundamentalist circles, with the most recent current events always being brought into prophetic line. It was a smug, antiestablishment creed, predicated on the utter corruption of all but the small remnant of the saved, and in the postwar period it had retreated before the more inclusive, mainstream evangelicalism of Billy Graham and his friends at the National Association of Evangelicals. Israel's capture of Jerusalem during the Six-Day War—which seemed to bring nearer the requisite renewal of Temple sacrifice—doubtless helped invigorate the cause of dispensational theology, but that alone cannot explain the astonishing sales of Lindsey's book. *The Late Great Planet Earth* offered the prospect of getting off the planet as abruptly and happily as possible—away from Vietnam and Cambodia, from Watergate and OPEC, from the Reverend Jim Jones and the Ayatollah Ruhollah Khomeini. In the backwash of the sixties, you didn't have to be born again to reach for notions of apocalypse now. The country was passing through a crisis of legitimacy, and Lindsey, unlike Graham, made no effort to reinvigorate the American myth. "It is clear," he wrote, "that the United States cannot be the leader of the West in the future." Thanks to student rebellion, Communist subversion, and wholesale moral decay, we would in all likelihood be relegated to a mere appendage of the Roman Antichrist. The American jeremiad had mutated into the latest revelation of Saint John the Divine.

Between the extremes of post–Judeo-Christian transcendence and pre–Judeo-Christian rapture, there was, finally, spiritual feminism, which swept through all the standard-brand churches during the 1970s. Its enemy was patriarchy; so rife with it was the Judeo-Christian tradition that the movement's most important manifesto, Mary Daly's *Beyond God the Father* (1973), treated Western faith as frankly unredeemable, and urged that the lost cause be abandoned. Although many religious feminists chose to stay and fight—flocking, indeed, into the seminaries—sisterhood became a powerful special consensus of its own. The mainline denominations struggled to adjust to the revolution in their ranks. But in the meantime, in quite another quarter, an adhesional counterrevolution was taking shape.

8 ▪ **A PLURAL MAJORITY**

``S T O P the RIPOFF of your rights! Cast a 'KNOW' vote," read the circular, with the "T" in "vote" printed as a large cross. On August 21, and 22, 1980, more than ten thousand people responded by turning up at Reunion Arena in Dallas to attend the National Affairs Briefing, an exercise in political bridge-building sponsored by the conservative Religious Roundtable. The bridge to be built went from secular right-wingers primarily concerned about defense, taxes, and government regulation of business to evangelical folk upset by legalized abortion, the Equal Rights Amendment, pornography, gay rights, and the banning of prayer from the public schools. Heretofore passive fundamentalists and charismatics were to be transformed, for the coming election, into political activists. "You'll walk away with know-how to inform and mobilize your church and community in a non-partisan drive to push beyond complaint into positive control of your destiny."

The spiritual politics was new; nonpartisan, however, it wasn't. When it was not featuring the ministerial likes of James Robison, Pat Robertson, Jerry Falwell, and Dallas' own W. A. Criswell, the program kept to the Republican straight-and-narrow: Jesse Helms, William Armstrong, Phil Crane, William Clements, John Connally. The voting records of all members of Congress were on display, and workshops were conducted on how to promote the exercise of a "Christian" franchise. ("Get 'em saved; get 'em baptized; get 'em registered," ran one slogan.) Highlighting the affair was the appearance of the Republican nominee for president, Ronald Reagan, as after-dinner speaker on the second day. "I know you cannot endorse me," Reagan told the crowd, "but I endorse you and everything you do." It was before dinner, however, while the candidate was holding a press conference across the way, that the briefing's most significant rhetorical event occurred. At the podium was Bailey Smith, pastor of the First Southern Baptist Church of Del City, Oklahoma, and recently elected president of the Southern Baptist Convention. Seized with the spirit of the occasion, Smith took it upon himself to deliver an aside on the place of religion in American electioneering:

> It is interesting at great political rallies how you have a Protestant to pray, and then you have a Catholic to pray, and then you have a Jew to pray. With all due respect to those dear people, my friend God Almighty does not hear the prayer of a Jew. For how in the world can God hear the prayer of a man who says that Jesus Christ is not the true Messiah. It is blasphemy. It may be politically expedient, but no one can pray unless he prays through the name of Jesus Christ. It is not Jesus among many, it is Jesus and Jesus only, it is Christ only, there is no competition for Jesus Christ.

Political expedience was not one of Smith's vices.

The remark did not attract immediate notice, because the reporters were out questioning Reagan and didn't hear it. But as happened, one of "those dear people," Director Milton Tobian of the Southwest region of the American Jewish Committee, had been in the audience taping the entire proceedings. After listening over and over to the offending words, Tobian prepared a transcript, and then a memo, both of which he circulated to a number of Jewish leaders around the country.

In his memo he described the briefing as "the first major public demonstration" of a movement capable of separating "American Jews from effective participation and influence in American decision making." As a liberal, Tobian was hostile to the briefing's domestic program, but what concerned him most was its overall "effort to promote 'Christian principles' by electing only those who subscribe rigidly to those principles." This, he thought, added up to "a call for a theocracy" in which the fundamentalists were "Theo," pluralism "a fossil memory," and the Jews "perforce" left out. Smith had merely been the one to make such exclusiveness overt. After receiving Tobian's transcript, Marc Tanenbaum, the director of interreligious affairs for the AJC in New York, decided (as he later recalled) that it was "extremely important to let Bailey Smith and the Bailey Smiths of the world know how really offensive this was to us." He had himself initiated interfaith discussions with Billy Graham and other prominent evangelicals back in the mid-1960s. "Our evangelical Christian friends had to know how we felt," he said, "so they would speak out." Accordingly, he released the transcript to the press, and on September 18 *The New York Times* ran a story telling what Smith had said and what various interested parties thought of it.

"Invincible ignorance" was Tanenbaum's own judgment (rendered in a Roman Catholic phrase specifying grounds for someone's being saved outside the Church). "The kindest thing I can say is that he knows nothing about Judaism and he is insensitive to his position as a spokesman for the largest Protestant denomination." As far as James Dunn of the Dallas-based Christian Life Commission of Texas Baptists was concerned, Smith had broken the traditional Baptist commitment to freedom of religion. "You can't really believe in religious liberty without respecting the religious convictions of others." Dunn also suggested that Smith was guilty of bad theology. "If God Almighty cannot hear the prayers of Jews, you're putting pretty severe limitations on your doctrine of God. I'm not willing to say what He can and what He cannot do." But while, in his view, Smith had made "sort of the ultimate anti-Semitic remark," the man himself denied it: "I am pro-Jew. I believe they are God's special people." Yet, he insisted, "without Jesus Christ they are lost. No prayer gets through that is not prayed through Jesus Christ. . . . Jews have an argument with me because they have an argument with the New Testament."[1]

What might Smith have known about Judaism to get him to change his mind? Could one respect others' religious convictions without believing them to be true? Should a fundamentalist preacher be obliged to hold that those who reject the divinity of his Lord and Saviour nevertheless enjoy access to the Godhead? In the midst of an election campaign fraught with tension over the role of religion in politics, such niceties seemed very much beside the point. A prominent Protestant had publicly pronounced one of the three legs of America's spiritual milking-stool to be unsound. He became forthwith a figure of national notoriety. "I could understand some camp preacher whose lack of knowledge would possibly excuse him," Tobian told the *Times*, "but this is the president of the Southern Baptist Convention." In fact, Smith's election to that post had been a victory for what amounted to the convention's camp-preacher wing, which had lately mobilized against what it considered moral and doctrinal laxity on the part of the Southern Baptist establishment. The affair gave moderates a chance to dissociate themselves from a leader they regarded with distaste, and hundreds of them wrote letters condemning this return, as they saw it, to theological Neanderthalism. Nor was Bailey Smith the only one to feel the heat.

Down in Lynchburg, Virginia, Jerry Falwell, the independent Baptist minister who, with his Moral Majority organization, had come to symbolize the irruption of fundamentalist Protestantism into American politics, looked as though he were trying to put some distance between himself and Smith when he told a reporter on October 1, "I believe that God answers the prayer of any redeemed Gentile or Jew and does not hear the prayers of unredeemed Gentiles or Jews." But when pressed for clarification, he declared that "redeemed means one who trusts in God through his faith in Jesus Christ," thus leaving little doubt where he stood on the question. Two days later, candidate Reagan himself showed up in Lynchburg to address a meeting of the Association of Religious Broadcasters and was asked to state *his* position on the efficacy of Jewish prayer. "Since both the Christian and Judaic religions are based on the same God, the God of Moses, I'm quite sure those prayers are heard," he said. "But then, I guess everyone can make his own interpretation of the Bible, and many individuals have been making differing interpretations for a long time." Falwell, when informed of these remarks, was understanding. The chief executive had to be "president of all the people," he said. "I would fight for his right to believe that. I appreciate his stand." His own education in the spiritual demands of national politics, however, remained to be completed.[2]

Lynchburg itself had presented political challenges for him, as Frances FitzGerald discovered when she paid the city a visit the following year for *The New Yorker*. Though born and raised there, Brother Falwell was something of an outsider, the creator of a community which kept itself apart. At Thomas Road Baptist Church, Liberty Baptist College, and Liberty Baptist Seminary, they were staunch puritanical dispensationalists, and the circumambient Lynchburgers, whom they subjected to continual proselytizing, had little use for them. Falwell's larger constituency comprised the devotees of the "Old Time Gospel Hour," a videotaped version of the weekly eleven o'clock service at Thomas Road, syndicated to television stations around the country. Yet the preacher had kept on good terms with Lynchburg's predominantly Episcopalian establishment. He was not above speaking to the Rotary Club or soliciting the help of the city's business leaders; nor would he denounce a Lynchburg plant for printing that organ of deviltry, *Penthouse* magazine. And when he decided to put himself before a wider public, he recognized that the old-time message of conversion he dispensed to his flock would require some adapting. During the bicentennial year he had mounted "I Love America" rallies on the steps of state capitols around the country, and these he revived in 1979 for the campaign against liberalism which featured Moral Majority, Inc., organized that year with the advice and counsel of professional right-wing lobbyists. The campaign's adhesional manifesto was Falwell's book *Listen, America!*; in 1980 it served as the counterstroke to the previous decade's *The Late Great Planet Earth*.[3]

Here was a dispensationalist author who had no intention of throwing in the national towel. *Listen, America!* (*cf.* Hear, O Israel!) was a cry for the repentance and revival that would return the land from the brink of ruin to its aboriginal pristine self. "God has blessed this nation because in its early days she sought to honor God and the Bible, the inerrant Word of the living God," wrote Falwell. Just as "our Founding Fathers firmly believed that America had a special destiny in the world," so he believed that America, with "more God-fearing citizens per capita than any other nation on earth," was the "last logical base for World evangelization." City on a Hill, New Jerusalem, Light unto the Gentiles—the American jeremiad was back in force. The spiritual politics was appropriately ecumenical. Falwell had created the Moral Majority to weld not only "Bible-believing Christians" but also other "concerned moral Americans" into a force capable of setting the country again on a firm biblical footing. What that required was a patriarchal family, with no new rights for women, children, or homosexuals; the abolition of legal abortion; tougher restrictions on pornography and drugs; increased military spending; and, dispensationally, unwavering support for the state of Israel. Politicians were to be judged according to how they voted on these issues. Falwell knew that his Baptist brethren had long been skittish about mixing religion and politics. (He had in his earlier days been skittish himself.) But now it was either stand up and be counted or face the children when they asked, "Mom and Dad, where were you the day freedom died in America?" A gospel, in short, for the Reagan dispensation.[4]

On October 6, 1980, amidst the commotion over Bailey Smith, Jimmy Allen, a politically liberal past president of the Southern Baptist Convention, staged an ecumenical press conference at the National Press Club in Washington to repudiate the "New Right Evangelicals"; the repudiation was issued— separately, jointly, and in no uncertain terms—by himself,

Charles V. Bergstrom of the Lutheran Council, Monsignor George G. Higgins of Catholic University, and Rabbi Tanenbaum. When Tanenbaum got back to his desk in New York, Jerry Falwell was on the line. He had just seen a report of the press conference on the AP wire and wanted the rabbi to know of his deep love for the Jewish people. He was going to be in New York in a couple of days. Could he come by for a chat?

Falwell began their hour-long meeting by brushing aside Smith's remark as something with which he did not agree. Be that as it might, said Tanenbaum, the New Right evangelicals were collectively engaged in a direct assault on religious pluralism. He then proceeded to deliver an impromptu lecture on how Baptists had struggled against the oppression of the Anglican establishment in colonial Virginia, how they had sacrificed life and limb for the principle of religious liberty ultimately embodied in the Bill of Rights. "You don't know your own history," he declared. "Tell me more," replied the minister from Lynchburg. After the lecture, Falwell professed true devotion to the principle of religious liberty. Would he, asked Tanenbaum, handing him a yellow pad, put that in writing? Yes, said Falwell, and under the rabbi's guidance fashioned a statement in which he asserted (somewhat oddly, in light of Acts 10:34) that God "is a respecter of all persons" who "loves everyone alike" and "hears the cry of any sincere person who calls on Him." He went on to say that a "very healthy relationship has been developing between Bible-believing Christians in America and the Jewish community," that he had "worked long and hard to enhance this relationship" and would continue to do so, and that it was a relationship which "transcends any political campaign." Summoning Americans of all faiths "to rise above every effort to polarize us in our efforts to return this nation to a commitment to the moral principles on which America was built," he said that America was and needed to remain "a pluralistic republic" and that "we must never allow" our "differing theological principles" to "separate us as Americans who love and respect each other as united people." A final paragraph, not part of the resulting press release but contained in the subsequent *Times* story, stated that the "alignment of evangelical Christians and Jews" would "withstand the slurs and political exploitation of these days."[5]

If the business about polarization and political exploitation seemed somewhat beside the point, that was because it was directed not at Bailey Smith but at President Jimmy Carter, the born-again candidate for reelection against whom the religious right had set its face. At the end of September, Carter had described the election of 1980 as one that would decide whether there would be an "alienation" of Christian and Jew; speaking in Chicago after Reagan's trip to Lynchburg, he claimed that voters faced a choice "if I lose the election, whether Americans might be separate, black from white, Jew from Gentile, North from South, rural from urban."[6] Even liberal editorialists considered these comments out of line, and Carter was forced to back off. With that, the "Jewish prayer issue" faded from view.

But loose ends remained, and after election day they began to be tied up. In mid-November, Bailey Smith himself, stung by the criticism from within his own flock, wrote to Nathan Perlmutter of the Anti-Defamation League of B'nai B'rith expressing "a great desire for better understanding with you and your people," and requesting a meeting; the following month he and other representatives of the Southern Baptist Convention made their way to New York and agreed to work together with the ADL to "improve communication." For his part, Smith apologized for any hurt he had caused, and affirmed his belief in a pluralistic American society. A few months later, he attended a Passover seder at the Plano, Texas, home of Mark Briskman, director of the North Texas–Oklahoma Anti-Defamation League, whom he had met in New York. Afterward, Briskman quoted him as saying, "I would die for your right to live as a Jew in America." Jewish-Baptist seminars and Sunday School lessons, even a joint trip to Israel, were set in train. "The ADL did a good piece of work," recalled the AJC's Tanenbaum, but only by way of "damage-control"; for despite the apology, Smith never took back the words that had caused all the fuss. The following June, after his reelection as president of the Southern Baptist Convention, he stated that "a person without Jesus is eternally lost." As for the prayers of Jews: "Everybody agrees this has had enough publicity." (In 1987, he received a standing ovation from the Conference of Southern Baptist Evangelists when he declared that he had not compromised on the subject. "If the Bible says it, it is true, and you should tell it," he said, noting that while he loved the Jewish people, "unless they repent and get born again, they are in trouble.")[7]

And yet, pace Tanenbaum, what damage had been done to the cause of religious pluralism in America? New interfaith relationships were forged, pledges of allegiance to the pluralist principle were elicited from those who seemed most to threaten it, and no one (except Jerry Falwell) felt impelled to trim his theological sails. Here, in short, was a textbook example of how to turn back a challenge to the standing religious order. Whatever the Bailey Smith affair itself signified, however, spiritual exclusivity was not the only thing about resurgent fundamentalism that unsettled American Jewry in 1980.

At the National Affairs Briefing, Jerry Falwell had (so Milton Tobian reported) "stated passionately that 'any nation, including the United States, which lifts up its hands against tiny Israel, surely will be destroyed.' " Afterward, CBS correspondent Bill Moyers had sought Tobian out, sensing that "my single issue was Israel." Surely, Moyers suggested, "with such an offer of powerful support, the rest of the agenda had been rendered palatable." Tobian demurred; pointing to two "Hebrew Christians" included in the program to testify about their conversion to Christianity, he noted that the same people who brought such glad tidings about Israel also separated Jews out as "unworthy of a valid God faith." A similar line was taken after the election by the Reform rabbi Alexander M. Schindler, in his presidential address to the Union of American Hebrew Congregations meeting in San Francisco. Calling on Christians and Jews to oppose the "chilling power of the radical right," Schindler singled out both Smith and Falwell for contributing (though perhaps not deliberately) to anti-Semitism—the one, by saying that only one brand of believers was acceptable to

God; the other, by saying that only one brand of politics was. The fundamentalists' support for Israel should not confuse the issue, said Schindler, for it was based on a doctrine of the Second Coming which required the ultimate conversion of Jews to Christianity. "They believe further that even devout Jews are not welcome in heaven."[8]

But not all Jewish leaders felt this way. Indeed, in response to Schindler's remarks, Perlmutter of the ADL took up cudgels in Falwell's behalf. Looking at the fundamentalists "as a monolithic group," he said, "is every bit as mischievous as viewing Jews or Catholics as a monolithic group. . . . I respectfully remind Rabbi Schindler that the Soviet Union, the prime exporter of anti-Semitism, is neither Christian nor fundamentalist." And Falwell himself pointed out that just two weeks before, he had received from Israeli Prime Minister Menachem Begin an award "in recognition of my many years of service to Israel and to the Jewish people everywhere." Returned Schindler, in a letter to the *Times*, "Mr. Falwell's support for Israel is welcome, of course, as is the support of anyone else. But it is irrelevant to the central question of the meaning and impact of the Moral Majority on the democratic process in America."[9]

How irrelevant was it? In his memo on the National Affairs Briefing, Tobian had warned that the religious right might well "shift the political center of gravity so far to the right that the traditional alliances in which Jews have been active become powerless and impotent." After Reagan and company's stunning defeat of those traditional alliances, Perlmutter, for one, was prepared to entertain the possibility of new coalitions. As he and his wife wrote in their 1982 tract *The Real Anti-Semitism in America*, "The preference Jews have manifested for the political Left over the Right requires reconsideration; characteristics of the socially conscious, modernist Christian denominations which traditionally comforted us and characteristics of the socially narrow-gauged Christian fundamentalists which traditionally discomforted us require our reevaluation; the mutuality of interests in our long-standing alliance with the Black civil-rights establishment is not as reciprocal as within easy memory it was." For the Perlmutters, "real anti-Semitism" was to be found in whatever impaired the real interests of Jews; and from affirmative action to the Soviet Union, Jewish interests seemed to them to lie increasingly with the right-wing positions.

But Israel was the touchstone of this proposed Jewish demarche from liberalism. How preferable was Falwell's resoluteness to the balancing act which the National Council of Churches performed in November of 1980, when it urged both that the Palestine Liberation Organization be recognized as the sole representative of the Palestinian people and that the PLO recognize the sovereignty of Israel. "The closer we have teamed with the liberal Protestant bodies," wrote the Perlmutters, "the farther have they moved from us on the issue central to our beings, Israel's security." Sure, the liberal Protestants were more benign theologically, but nowadays that didn't count for much. "Christian-professing religious attitudes, in this time, in this country, are for all practical purposes, no more than personally held religious conceits, barely impacting the way in which Jews live. Their political action, as it relates to the security of the state of Israel, impacts us far more meaningfully than whether a Christian neighbor believes that his is the exclusive hot line to 'on high.' " As for those fundamentalist Christian neighbors who embraced Israel in expectation of the Second Coming and the conversion of the Jews, the Perlmutters were prepared to assume an agnostic posture. "If the Messiah comes, on that very day we'll consider our options. Meanwhile, let's praise the Lord and pass the ammunition." [10]

Such blitheness, however vulgarly expressed, may well have been in order; after all, even a Bailey Smith could be persuaded to play by the prevailing rules of interreligious comity. (It is worth noting that Smith, in his original remark, had not found fault with Roman Catholic prayers—a remarkable testimony to just how far the spirit of Christian ecumenicity had penetrated the fundamentalist mind.) Yet what the Perlmutters disclosed was less a sense of theological unconcern than a sensitivity to new power realities. The "religious conceits" of the Christian rightists could scarcely be dissociated from their political activities. The point was, they were the Protestant force that had to be reckoned with.

If the right-wing Christians were feeling their oats politically, it was because they had reason to believe that, within American Protestantism anyway, their day had come. The alarm had been sounded in 1972 by Dean Kelley, an official of the National Council of Churches, in a book called *Why the Conservative Churches Are Growing;* by chart and graph Kelley showed that one after another, the "liberal" mainline churches were in decline—in terms of membership, church-building, missionary work, periodical subscriptions, you name it. By contrast, the Southern Baptists and the Mormons and the Assemblies of God and the Jehovah's Witnesses were growing apace. Kelley's explanation was that these bodies offered their members a "strong" faith, in contrast to the bland product of the great denominations of the Protestant establishment. The contrast, of course, had been around since 1958, when Henry P. Van Dusen first called attention to the "third force" in Christianity. But it was one thing to flog the complacent throngs in the suburban churches with someone else's profound spiritual commitment, quite another to see it as triumphing in the recruitment battle for American hearts and souls.

Kelley's explanation did not go unchallenged, including by some who contended that progressive politics, not namby-pambiness, was responsible for alienating mainline churchgoers; and a good thing too. That made sense to the conservatives, whose practice it was to charge the establishment with selling its birthright for a mess of feminist, Third World, and homosexual pottage. Later sociological studies suggested that Kelley may have underestimated such "contextual" factors as population shifts to the South and West, where the conservative denominations were thicker on the ground: if you moved from Akron to Forth Worth, the church you joined down the street was just more likely to be Southern Baptist. Mainline denominations had, moreover, been surrendering "market share" to the conservatives right along since 1920; there was no cause for alarm. But whatever the context, by the end of the 1970s most observers seemed to agree that the place to find Protestant church commitment was, in the words of the sociologists of religion Hoge and Roozen, "mainly in a gradually shrinking sector of the culture anchored at the traditional evangelical pole."[11]

Certainly that was where the action was. When Harvey Cox returned in 1984 to the political concerns that had animated *The Secular City*, his hopes lay with spiritual modalities far removed from the desacralized urban piety of two decades before. The theologian of the New Frontier had, in the intervening years, been through a lot. In 1969 he'd opened his heart to the counterculture, urging a religion of more fun and games in *The Feast of Fools*. In 1973, *The Seduction of the Spirit* had quested after "people's religion"—varieties of popular religious experience ranging from the author's own Quaker-Baptist childhood in Pennsylvania to peasant adoration of the Virgin in Mexico to self-actualization in the fleshpots of Big Sur. Nineteen seventy-seven found Cox turning east in *Turning East*. *Religion in the Secular City*, his treatise for the 1980s, fixed its gaze on the "base communities" of liberation theology in Latin America and on fundamentalism here at home. Cox may have rejected the fundamentalist political agenda, but he appreciated its spiritual energies. When progressive North American Christians like himself got around to developing their own liberation theology and base communities, these would, he felt, "emerge more readily from the evangelical-conservative than from the liberal wing of American Christianity. We need a liberation theology that will draw on the folk piety of Baptists, Methodists, and the rest."[12]

For its part, the Christian right worked on its own strategy of national liberation. Since the early days of Youth for Christ, American evangelicals had known how to combine patriotism with spiritual uplift; but the new breed tended to have the field to itself. The Henry Luces and John Foster Dulleses were gone from the scene, and in the wake of the Watergate scandal even a still active Billy Graham, chastened for his misplaced faith in Richard Nixon, no longer went in for enthusiastic flag-waving. Communism, though it remained the principal foreign bogey, was supplanted domestically by the tyrant of "secular humanism," on whose shoulders reposed responsibility for all the changes in moral norms that had come upon American society since "the sixties." In the ecumenical cosmology of the Christian right, secular humanism had pledged itself to destroy nothing other than . . . well, in May of 1983, the tabloid of the Moral Majority reported "a systematic pattern of discrimination against . . . [books] which display philosophical positions rooted in the Judeo-Christian tradition." [13]

Such right-wing ecumenism was bona fide; or at least, there was no reason to suppose Jerry Falwell any less sincere than, say, the politically sensitive Perlmutters when he reached out to Catholics and Orthodox Jews for support on issues like abortion, homosexual rights, and pornography. If the Judeo-Christian tradition had earlier been a witness for civil rights, it now served the cause of "traditional values." Yet fighting discrimination in the name of this religious heritage was one thing; using it to reverse the secular-humanist tide quite another. Given that the American Constitution forbade an establishment of religion, how could secular humanism be driven out of public life when what it stood for was a process of clearing the culture of religious "establishments"—proscriptions and practices like blue laws and antisodomy laws and prayers in school? Wasn't secular humanism just a name for constitutionally warranted disestablishment?

Not necessarily. Early in March of 1987, U.S. District Judge W. Brevard Hand enjoined the Alabama public schools from using forty-four textbooks in social studies, American history, and home economics on the ground that such use had illegally established a "religion of secular humanism." The judge pointed out that the Supreme Court had (for example, in conscientious-objection cases) recognized nontheistic convictions as religious; and he was able to identify self-described "humanists" gathered in organizations like the Ethical Culture Society and professing creeds like the Humanist Manifesto I and II. Secular humanism was therefore a religion; and as far as the social-studies and history books were concerned, it had been established through a discriminatory omission of references to "theistic religion" and the part it played in human affairs. ("In the course of American history, Judeo-Christianity occupies the major role within the theistic religious tradition.

Thus discrimination against theistic religion within American history texts occurs if this tradition is ignored or neglected.") A latter-day Mencken might have contended that the best possible case for secular humanism was an honest account of religious history; regardless, the judge aimed to enlarge the coverage of Judeo-Christianity in Alabama's history and social-studies courses.

The home-economics books, though, presented a different problem, for theirs were sins of actual commission. According to Judge Hand, they contained overt "antitheistic teachings" as well as statements advancing belief in "subjective and personal values without an external standard of right and wrong" and "hedonistic, pleasure, need-satisfaction motivation—the presumptive tenets of the secular humanist faith. Among the objectionable passages were:

- "Nothing was 'meant to be.' You are the designer of your life."
- "People who have strong prejudices are called bigots. Bigots are devoted to their own church, party or belief and will not consider the right of others to have varying opinions."
- "If a theist (one who believes a god exists) marries an atheist (one who denies the existence of a god), they may have some adjustment problems."
- "People of all races and cultural backgrounds should be shown as having high ideals and goals."
- "Each person is free to choose his or her lifestyle. With this freedom comes responsibility. You are responsible for your own life."
- "You may find that you have to tolerate differences in your peers as you learn to choose your own values because they are right for you."
- "Divorce is becoming more common in our society. Many couples are deciding that they have problems and differences they cannot resolve. They believe they would be happier living apart, so they get a divorce."
- "Self-actualization is the highest level of human need."

If these, when taught in the public schools, represented an establishment of religion, then the Constitution itself took on the appearance of a secular humanist document, promoting the belief that individuals should decide for themselves what to believe. Indeed, since the First Amendment was, in the judge's own words, "a guardian of personal freedom," there was no small irony in his employing it to prevent the state from teaching personal freedom as a value. Such instruction might be supposed to serve a purely secular, as opposed to a "secular humanist," purpose (such as the better functioning of democratic institutions); and that was one of the Supreme Court's criteria for determining the admissibility of government action under the First Amendment. But wouldn't inculcating this value at the same time constitute an establishment of religion?

> Mere coincidence between a statement in a textbook and a religious belief [wrote the judge] is not an establishment of religion. However, some religious beliefs are so fundamental that the act of denying them will completely undermine that religion. In addition, denial of that belief will result in the affirmance of a contrary belief and result in the establishment of an opposing religion.

Those seeking a return to traditional values were thus caught on the horns of a dilemma. If the laissez-faire culture of the time was actually the expression of an alien, anti–Judeo-Christian faith, then it could be excluded from American public institutions. But if it were thus excluded, then so would be any expression of other religions which denied its beliefs. Secular humanists would be able to petition to have references to an external standard of right and wrong removed from textbooks as prejudicial to their faith. The state would therefore be compelled to get out of the business of moral education altogether —a victory, presumably, for secular humanism, and just the opposite of what many conservative religionists seemed to have in mind.[14]

One way to avoid this conundrum was proposed by Richard Neuhaus, the onetime scourge of the Vietnam war now emerged as a neoconservative. In *The Naked Public Square*

(1984), Neuhaus lamented that between mainline Protestantism's loss of cultural hegemony and recent secularizing rulings
of the courts, religion had lost its voice in the affairs of state.
Democracy, "a fragile and imperiled artifice," required that
voice; for "without a transcendent or religious point of reference, conflicts of values cannot be resolved." This recalled the
intellectuals who, after World War II, had cried out that democracy without religion could not inspire American citizens
to a defense of the West; like them, Neuhaus appealed to an
ecumenical faith, a "Judeo-Christian consensus." Yet in
beckoning religion back into the public square, he was notably
unspecific about what that consensus consisted of—possibly
because it was not, on any given issue, so easy to determine.
The abortion question, his prime exhibit for a current unresolved conflict of values, was clearly resolved neither by Scripture nor by the history of Western moral legislation. What
Neuhaus seemed to be calling for, however, was less a set of
Judeo-Christian policy recommendations than the reestablish-
ment of "a shared world of moral discourse." The moral ma-
joritarians had "kicked a tripwire" alerting all Americans to
the consequences of abandoning a "religiously based moral
common denominator."[15]

If this was the neoconservative plaint, the neoliberal one
could be found in Habits of the Heart, a sociological inquiry
into contemporary American values by Robert Bellah and several collaborators. Bellah's own view of the country's collective faith had soured considerably since the time he had
looked to it for rescue from the war in Vietnam; in the wake of
the Watergate affair, he decided that the American civil religion had become "an empty and broken shell." Habits sought
not a civil religious revival so much as "an effective public
church in the United States today, bringing the concerns of
biblical religion into the common discussion." This was
needed to reestablish a sense of community and social commitment; it offered "the major alternative in our culture to
radical religious individualism on the one hand and what
[Martin] Marty calls 'religious tribalism' on the other." In fact,
the tribal preoccupations of the fundamentalist churches wor-

ried Bellah et al. far less than the privatized faith of religious isolates—exemplified for them in a young nurse named Sheila Larson. "I believe in God," she reported. "I'm not a religious fanatic. I can't remember the last time I went to church. My faith has carried me a long way. It's Sheilaism. Just my own little voice. . . . It's just try to love yourself and be gentle with yourself. You know, I guess, take care of each other. I think He would want us to take care of each other." Two experiences defined this "Sheilaist'" faith:

> One occurred just before she was about to undergo major surgery. God spoke to her to reassure her that all would be well, but the voice was her own. The other experience occurred when, as a nurse, she was caring for a dying woman whose husband was not able to handle the situation. Taking over care in the final hours, Sheila had the experience that "if she looked in the mirror" she "would see Jesus Christ."[16]

In Sheila Larson the authors had stumbled upon an incarnation of what William James, at the end of *The Varieties of Religious Experience*, had judged to be the minimum requirements of functioning religion: "the belief that beyond each man and in a fashion continuous with him there exists a larger power which is friendly to him and to his ideals."

> All that the facts require is that the power should be both other and larger than our conscious selves. Anything larger will do, if only it be large enough to trust for the next step. It need not be infinite, it need not be solitary. It might conceivably even be only a larger and more godlike self, of which the present self would then be but the mutilated expression, and the universe might conceivably be a collection of such selves, of different degrees of inclusiveness, with no absolute unity realized in it at all. Thus would a sort of polytheism return upon us.

Such polytheism, which James considered to have "always been the real religion of common people," was antipathetic to the "monistic view" that "unless there be one all-inclusive God, our guarantee of security is left imperfect," and "our religious consolation would . . . fail to be complete."[17] But in the spiritual variety show of the late twentieth century, it was a view worth considering. What if Bailey Smith had been understood to say no more than "My sect's particular deity won't help those who do not acknowledge him"? What if no single spiritual umbrella needed to be placed over the Rajneeshees of Rajneeshpuram and the Mormons of Salt Lake, the hasidim of Williamsburg and the fundamentalists of Lynchburg, the presidential candidate who claimed to control the weather with prayer and the "channelers" who claimed to be in touch with prehistoric and alien beings? What if a simple polytheistic conclusion were inferred from the "flat anarchy" which in his day Emerson descried in the country's "ecclesiastic realms"? Would the world as Americans knew it come to an end?

Yet how could James's pluralistic universe appeal to a society predicated on "Nature's God," a society whose major religious traditions, if they prided themselves on anything, prided themselves on their monotheism? In public, Americans insisted that they worshiped the same God, whatever that meant; and when a Bailey Smith spoke up, the question perforce was whether that god listened to only certain of his devotees. Ecumenically minded theologians would contend that it was not for mere mortals to say whom the Absolute could or could not listen to, could or could not save. That might no more than beg the question of the transcendent, unbound nature of the divine; but perhaps it was enough to believe that our several monotheisms were headed toward some common understanding, or toward at least some final day of reckoning. Theologically, the adhesional demands of American civil society were rarely pressed further than that.

In *Protestant Catholic Jew*, Will Herberg guessed that America would be transformed from a nation of ethnic groups into a threefold religious order. Although he underestimated the persistence of ethnic particularism, he recognized—possibly because his ethnic group *was* a religion—that ethnicity would provide the model for whatever constituted cultural pluralism in the future. According to the literary historian Werner Sollors, American ethnic identity has relied on complementary portions of *descent* and *consent*: Americans are not only what their grandfathers were, but what they choose to be, and the ideal they strive for is a "properly ethnic" middle ground between the undesirable poles of ethnocentrism and deracination.[18] The same goes for religion; a properly religious American should be perched between fanaticism and indifference, maintaining a healthy integration of conversional and adhesional personas. In Budd Schulberg's 1952 terms, whoever throws over "the ways of his father" had better acquire a "sense of obligation to the Judeo-Christian pattern," lest he be left, like Sammy Glick, with nothing except "naked self-interest to guide himself." The supposed danger of secular humanist education was that it threatened to sever children from the ways of their families, leaving them with nothing to guide themselves but naked self-actualization. The American struggle with pluralism has been going on, *mutatis mutandis*, for a long time.

Moralists are not in business to point out how cultures manage to pass on their values and ensure their survival. If Judge Hand was concerned that public education was making the self into an idol, then so was the secular social critic Christopher Lasch when he denounced "the culture of competitive individualism, which in its decadence has carried the logic of individualism to the extreme of a war of all against all, the pursuit of happiness to the dead end of a narcissistic preoccupation with self."[19] Was the culprit secular humanism? Was it Philip Rieff's "triumph of the therapeutic"? Or was it, perhaps, the country's own evangelical Protestant tradition? In the eighteenth century, preachers of revival had abandoned predestinarian Calvinism in favor of the Arminian view that God's sovereign will could be coerced by human effort, that a person cooperated in the work of his redemption, that the individual was responsible for making himself whole. In the 1980s, neither American individualism nor its prophetically inclined assailants seemed likely to give up the fight.

Yet as the decade waned, the evangelical thunder appeared to be receding. Even in its heyday—when it had helped elect a president and push a half-dozen Democratic senators out of office in 1980—the Christian right had been a disputed political force; polls showed that evangelical Protestants constituted no single voting bloc. By the time the elections of 1986 returned the Senate to the Democrats, Jerry Falwell had put the Moral Majority on hold and largely withdrawn from secular politics; his public backing now did candidates more harm than good. For him, at any rate, the inclusive spiritual crusade had fallen short. Despite the wishes of some of their neoconservative leaders, Jews continued to cleave to their traditional liberal politics. Out of the alliance between religious conservatives and secular right-wingers, the former had gotten little but rhetorical encouragement from both Reagan administrations on abortion, prayer in schools, and the other issues that mattered most to them; while the latter had to contend, in 1988, with the unwanted presidential candidacy of the Reverend Pat Robertson.

There were signs, moreover, that American religion was slouching back to normalcy. Membership in the mainline churches, whose decline had provoked such consternation in the 1970s, stabilized and even started to creep upward again. Demographic statistics suggested that the creatures of the postwar baby boom, after abandoning traditional religious practice in droves, were finding their way back to more familiar altars. Rebels in the sixties, singles in the seventies, they had finally buckled down to family life; it turned out that joining the local church and depositing one's offspring in its Sunday school still came naturally to middle-class America.[20] Indeed, the phylogeny of the entire culture seemed chained to the ontogeny of this oversized generational organism, for the last time there had been a major upswing in the churchgoing population was when it had itself been in need of the Sunday-school experience.

Other shades of the postwar revival included a best-selling Boston rabbi, Harold Kushner, whose *When Bad Things Happen to Good People* recalled Joshua Loth Liebman's *Peace of Mind*; in place of the positive-thinking Norman Vincent Peale in New York's Marble Collegiate Church there was the possibility-thinking Robert Schuller in Garden Grove, California's,

Crystal Cathedral. The Protestant establishment might not yet have recaptured the public ear, but the Roman Catholic bishops showed that a mainline faith could attract unexampled public attention with pronouncements on nuclear weapons and the economic system. A consensus was even building on the advisability of including more information on religion in the public-school curriculum, and more teaching of "values." Was it time for a Fifth Great Awakening? Would *Partisan Review* spring to life with a symposium on a new new *new* failure of nerve? Would worries about excessive pluralism blow away in a bluster of revived concern over conventional piety?

And if adhesional faith was reviving to the left of the religious right, by what name would it be called? Liberal gentiles had long since learned to be wary of the Judeo-Christian tradition. To the feminist theologian Rosemary Ruether it was simply a disguise for a history of Christian anti-Semitism; the socialist author Michael Harrington felt obliged to insist that it did not *have* to be "a device to assimilate an authentic Judaism to an arrogant Christianity"; and Martin Marty, alert to recent right-wing appropriations, took to the pages of *The Christian Century* to condemn what "is often a code word for those promoting a Christian America." At the same time, the sociological usefulness of "Judeo-Christian" as a description of American society seemed more dubious than ever. As of 1985, noted Wade Clark Roof and William McKinney, "a heterogeneous assortment of non–Judeo-Christian faiths" commanded the loyalties of twice the number of Americans Judaism did, while nearly one American in ten reported no affiliation with any religious faith; three decades earlier, the nonreligious and the non–Judeo-Christian had together constituted a mere 3 percent of the population. "Jews feel to an extent co-opted by the expansion of the notion of teaching the Christian tradition into the notion of teaching the Judeo-Christian tradition," said David Gordis, executive vice president of the American Jewish Committee, in 1987. "Our view of America is of a society which is truly pluralistic, one which continues to create and re-create its value system on the basis of the insights and the perspectives, not only of Christians and Jews, but of Moslems and of those who believe in Eastern religions. Each of these groups as they come to this country must contribute to the shaping of consensus. It's an evolving tradition of values." Perhaps, after all, it was best to bid Judeo-Christian America adieu.[21]

And still. . .

In 1974 the sociologist John Murray Cuddihy published a study of "the Jewish struggle with modernity" called *The Ordeal of Civility*. Like Arthur Cohen before him, Cuddihy considered the idea of a Judeo-Christian civilization mere "ecumenist public relations" whose popularity bore witness to "the cultural and theological illiteracy of our times." His heroes were "the great unassimilated, implacable Jews of the West"—by which he meant not Zionists or hasidim, but "proud pariahs" like Marx, Freud, and Claude Lévi-Strauss, who represented "a principled and stubborn resistance to the whole western 'thing.' " Unfortunately, however, most Jewish intellectuals had succumbed to the gentilities of a Western civilization that was nothing else than "an incognito or secularized form of Christianity."[22]

Thus, in late-twentieth-century America, did a lapsed Irish Catholic Jeremiah of the academy summon Jewish colleagues to overthrow individualistically the idols of their tribe. There could be, in Western civilization, few odder injunctions to keep the faith; and few more striking testimonies to the persistence, under whatever name, of the Judeo-Christian tradition in American life.

■ NOTES

INTRODUCTION

1. Ralph Waldo Emerson, "Worship," *The Conduct of Life* (Boston and New York, 1904), 203–4, 208–9.

2. Sidney E. Mead, *The Old Religion in the Brave New World: Reflections on the Relation between Christendom and the Republic* (Berkeley, 1977), 2.

3. Arthur Darby Nock, *Conversion: The Old and the New in Religion from Alexander the Great to Augustine of Hippo* (Oxford, 1933), 7.

4. See Robert T. Handy, "The American Religious Depression," *Religion in American History*, eds. J. M. Mulder and J. F. Wilson (Englewood Cliffs, N.J., 1978), 441.

CHAPTER 1

1. *New York Times*, August 10, 1945.

2. Quoted in Martin J. Sherwin, "Hiroshima and Modern Memory," *The Nation*, October 10, 1981; *New York Times*, August 25, 1945.

3. *Christian Century* LXII, 923; *New York Times*, August 20, 1945; Paul Hutchinson, *The New Leviathan* (Chicago, 1946), 49.

4. *Report of the Calhoun Commission* (1946), 12–13.

5. *New York Times*, August 8 and 9, 1945.

6. John K. Jessup, ed., *The Ideas of Henry Luce* (New York, 1969), 297.

7. Quoted in Michael J. Yavenditti, "American Reactions to the Use of Atomic Bombs on Japan, 1945–1947 (unpublished dissertation, University of California), chapter 4.

8. Cited in Hutchinson, *op. cit.*, 180; Rexford Tugwell, *A Chronicle of Jeopardy, 1945–55* (Chicago, 1958), 35–36.

9. Lewis Mumford, *Program for Survival* (New York, 1946), 122–25.

10. Dwight Macdonald. "The Root Is Man," *Politics* III (1946), 205, 100.

11. "Gentlemen: You Are Mad!" *Saturday Review of Literature*, March 30, 1946, 5; Milton Mayer, "Thomists and Atomists," *Common Sense*, November, 1945, 27–28; "God, Man and the Atom Bomb," *Catholic World* 163 (1946), 149; forum on "The Future of Religion," *American Scholar* 15 (1945–46), 110.

12. David Riesman, *Individualism Reconsidered* (Glencoe, Ill., 1954), 391; *Partisan Review* 17 (1950), 103, 333.

13. *New York Herald Tribune* Book Review, March 31, 1946; Joshua Loth Liebman, *Peace of Mind* (New York, 1946), 202, 173, 199.

14. (New York, 1948), 96.

15. George S. Stevenson, "The Antidote for Atomic Jitters," *New York Times Magazine*, May 13, 1951; for an insightful history of Mind Cure, see Donald Meyer, *The Positive Thinkers* (New York, 1965).

16. Pierre Lecompte du Nouy, *Human Destiny* (New York, 1947), 205, 273; Arnold Toynbee, *An Outline to History* (New York, 1947), 554.

17. "The 'Real' Reason," *McCall's*, February–April, 1947.

18. Fulton Sheen, *Peace of Soul* (New York, 1949), 14–15.

19. *The Seven Storey Mountain* (New York, 1948), 163–64.

20. *Partisan Review* 17 (1950), 480.

21. William G. McLoughlin, Jr., *Billy Graham: Revivalist in a Secular Age* (New York, 1960), 22.

CHAPTER 2

1. Budd Schulberg, *What Makes Sammy Run?* (New York, 1952), xiv; Patrick Henry, " 'And I Don't Care What It Is': The Tradition-History of a Civil Religion Proof-Text," *The Journal of the American Academy of Religion* 49 (1981), 41.

2. "Lector" (*nom de plume* of author), "Incense and Lights," *Literary Guide*, 20 N.S., October 1, 1899, 61; Joseph Freeman, *An American Testament* (New York, 1936), 61; George Orwell, "Sten-

dhal," *New English Weekly* 15 (July 27, 1939), 237; see John Roy Carlson (pseudonym of Arthur Derounian), *Under Cover: My Four Years in the Nazi Underworld of America* (Philadelphia and New York, 1943); Beatrice Jenney, ed., *Protestants Answer Anti-Semitism* (New York, 1941), inside front cover.

3. Carl J. Friedrich, "Anti-Semitism: Challenge to Christian Culture," in Isacque Graeber and Stewart Henderson Britt, eds., *Jews in a Gentile World: The Problems of Anti-Semitism* (New York, 1942), 7–8; Jacques Maritain, *Christianisme et démocratie* (New York, 1943), 29. An English translation of this essay was issued by Scribner's the following year.

4. *Science, Philosophy and Religion* IV (New York, 1944), 620; V (1945), 918, 919, 932, 957; IV, 753; V, 685, 924; VI (1947), 702; III (1943), 279, 287, 290; V, 926; VII (1947), 398, 402; II (1942), 255, 412, 541; III, 287; V, 928.

5. "The New Failure of Nerve," *Partisan Review* 10 (1943), 20.

6. Julian Morgenstern, "Judaism's Contribution to Post-War Religion," Hebrew Union College pamphlet (n.p. [1942]), 5, 15. This was Morgenstern's address inaugurating the college's 1942–43 academic year. Trude Weiss-Rosmarin, *Judaism and Christianity: The Differences* (New York, 1943), 11.

7. *Science, Philosophy and Religion* 10 (1950), 460; Patrick Henry, *op. cit.*, 41; *New York Times*, October 29, 1951, 26; July 23, 1952, 6.

8. Reinhold Niebuhr, Introd. to Waldo Frank, *The Jew in Our Day* (New York, 1944), 4; *The Nature and Destiny of Man* (New York, 1949) II, 36–37; *The Self and the Dramas of History* (New York, 1955), 44.

9. Matthew Arnold, *Culture and Anarchy* (1869, rpt. New York, 1941), 129–30; Niebuhr, *The Self and the Dramas of History*, 76, 117, 121, 160.

10. Paul Tillich, "Reinhold Niebuhr's Doctrine of Knowledge," in Charles W. Kegley and Robert W. Bretall, eds., *Reinhold Niebuhr: His Religious, Social, and Political Thought* (New York, 1956); Tillich from an unpublished manuscript quoted in A. Roy Eckardt, *Christianity and the Children of Israel* (New York, 1948), 146–47; Tillich, "Is There a Judeo-Christian Tradition?" *Judaism* 1 (1952), 107.

11. Niebuhr, *The Self and the Dramas of History*, 91; Eckardt, *op. cit.*, 146–47.

12. Frank, *op. cit.*, 181–82, 178, 184; *Partisan Review* 17 (1950), 234.

13. Abraham Heschel, "A Hebrew Evaluation of Reinhold Nie-

buhr," in Kegley and Bretall, *op. cit.*, 409; Herberg gave an account of his Niebuhrian conversion in a short article on Niebuhr, "Christian Apologist to the Secular World," *Union Seminary Quarterly Review* 11 (1956), 12; Bernhard W. Anderson, Introd. to Will Herberg, *Faith Enacted as History: Essays in Biblical Theology* (Philadelphia, 1976), 108.

14. Will Herberg, *Judaism and Modern Man* (Philadelphia, 1951), ix, xi; "Judaism and Christianity: Their Unity and Differences," in Herberg, *Faith Enacted as History*, 51. (Rosenzweig [1886–1929] was, like Herberg, a secularized Jew who flirted with Christianity before returning to the faith of his fathers; his conception of the relationship between Judaism and Christianity [summarized by Herberg] was most fully spelled out in his 1921 masterpiece, *Der Stern der Erlösung [The Star of Redemption].*) Herberg, *Judaism and Modern Man*, 61; *Protestant Catholic Jew* (Garden City, N.Y., 1960), ch. 11, 254–72.

15. Robert Gordis, *Judaism for the Modern Age* (New York, 1955), 216–17, 128; Alexander J. Burnstein, "Niebuhr, Scripture, and Normative Judaism," in Kegley and Bretall, eds., *Reinhold Niebuhr*, 412; Bernard Heller, "About the Judeo-Christian Tradition," *Judaism* 1 (1952), 260–61.

16. Niebuhr, *The Nature and Destiny of Man*, 145; *The Self and the Dramas of History*, 103; John Courtney Murray, *We Hold These Truths* (New York, 1960),138, 125.

17. Murray, *op cit.*, 138, 125; *Partisan Review* 17 (1950), 324. An extended discussion of "the Judeo-Christian revelation" occurs in Maritain's *Moral Philosophy* (New York, 1964), 75–91.

18. "Pray for the Jews," *America* 101, April 11, 1959, 215; Quentin Lauer, "Love Links Christian with Jew," *America* 94 (February 11, 1956), 530. See also the editors' Statement of Purpose in the first volume of *The Bridge* (New York, 1955), 9; Lauer, *ibid.*, 529.

19. Peter DeVries, *The Tunnel of Love* (Harmondsworth, 1982, 1st ed., 1954), 205.

CHAPTER 3

1. Jordan A. Schwartz, *The Speculator: Bernard M. Baruch in Washington, 1917–1965* (Chapel Hill, 1981), 560.

2. Wilson and Graham quotations in Marshall Frady, *Billy Graham: A Parable of American Righteousness* (Boston, 1979), 241–42; for Howland's recollection, see W. A. Swanberg, *Luce and His Empire* (New York, 1972), 290–91.

3. *Charlotte Observer*, October 27, 1957 (cited in William G. McLoughlin, Jr., *Billy Graham: Revivalist in a Secular Age* [New York, 1960], 238, n. 10).

4. Quoted in McLoughlin, *op. cit*, 3–4.

5. *Christian Century* 60 (1943), 596, 614.

6. Carl F. H. Henry, *The Uneasy Conscience of Modern Fundamentalism* (Grand Rapids, 1947), 81; see *Christian Century* 65 (1948), 104–5.

7. *Ibid*, 68 (1951), 536; James Kenneth Miller, correspondence with W. J. H. McKnight (1954, 1956), Presbyterian Historical Society, Philadelphia, Pa.

8. *Christian Century* 68 (1951), 536; 69 (1952), 543; 70 (1953), 551; 69 (1952), 494–96; 68 (1951), 814; 71 (1954), 357.

9. John C. Bennett, "Billy Graham at Union," *Union Seminary Quarterly Review* IX (May, 1954), 9–14.

10. See David P. Gaines, *The World Council of Churches* (Peterborough, N.H., 1966), 629–39, 1175–81.

11. *National Council Outlook* 4 (June, 1954), 19; Berlyn V. Farris, "Report to the Joint Department of Evangelism of the National Council of Churches," Archives of the National Council of Churches, Presbyterian Historical Society, Philadelphia, Pa. (hereafter NCA).

12. Sermon printed in Billy Graham, *Revival in Our Time* (Wheaton, Ill., 1950), 69–80.

13. See Sacvan Bercovitch, *The American Jeremiad* (New York, 1981).

14. From Graham's radio show, "Hour of Decision," "America's Decision," August, 1953.

15. *America's Hour of Decision* (Wheaton, Ill., 1951), 139–48.

16. *Ibid.*, 142; Frady, *op. cit.*, 240.

17. "Peace in Our Time" (Minneapolis, 1952); "Three Minutes to Twelve" (Minneapolis, 1953).

18 McLoughlin, *op. cit.*, 24.

CHAPTER 4

1. So committed was Coolidge to rapprochement between Yankee and Irish that although he was a pillar of Boston's fabled Watch and Ward Society, he even made a place at High Table for Brahmindom's arch-nemesis, Mayor James Michael Curley.

2. Dulles, "Leonard Feeney: In Memoriam," *America* 138 (February 25, 1978), 135.

3. Robert Conner (pseud. of Robert Colopy), *Walled In: The True Story of a Cult* (New York, 1979), 253.

4. Catherine Clarke, *The Loyolas and the Cabots* (Boston, 1950), 45; *Harvard Crimson*, December 6, 1951.

5. Avery Dulles, "On Keeping the Faith," *From the Housetops* I, 1 (1946), 60–62; Margaret T. O'Brien, "Secularism in American Colleges," *ibid.*, 40.

6. Arthur M. Schlesinger, Jr., *Robert Kennedy and His Times* (New York, 1978), 66.

7. "The Catholic Parent and the Catholic School," *Sermons and Addresses* X (Boston, 1931), 51–53; pamphlet of the Massachusetts Committee in the collection of Andover Library, Harvard University; *From the Housetops*, I, 2 (December, 1946), 5–6.

8. *Boston Globe*, February 16, 1948.

9. *Boston Globe*, August 9, 1948.

10. Mark Amory, ed., *The Letters of Evelyn Waugh* (Harmondsworth, 1982), 292–93.

11. *American Ecclesiastical Review* 127 (1952), 307–15.

12. There were defectors. In the early 1960s one of them, Robert Colopy, took his estranged wife and the rest of the slaves to court in order to gain custody of his sons, thus providing outsiders with a glimpse of life within this little world. (One of the sons, who himself defected from the group as a young man, wrote an account of his experiences under the pseudonym Robert Conner. See note 3.) Mrs. Clarke, than whom there was no stauncher defender of the Feeneyite faith, managed the center's day-to-day administration until her death in 1968. Not long thereafter, a process of reconciliation began. Humberto Cardinal Madeiros, who succeeded Cushing as archbishop of Boston in 1970, had as a young seminarian frequented the center before it was cast into outer darkness. He and others were unhappy at the prospect that someone convinced of the necessity of the Church for salvation would himself die outside it; if Roman Catholicism after Vatican II was commodious enough for a radical like Hans Küng, it ought to have a place for the ultraconservative Leonard Feeney. John Wright, now Roman cardinal in charge of all Catholic clergy, did his part to arrange the prodigal's return. No recantation was required, only a simple profession of faith; and in 1972 Feeney was received back into the Church. Some of his followers followed him back; others remained unreconciled. He ministered to his now divided flock until he died, in 1978. The reconciled affiliated themselves with established monastic orders, male and female, as St. Benedict's Priory.

13. Joseph Dever, *Cushing of Boston: A Candid Portrait* (Boston, 1965), 147.

14. Richard P. McBrien, *Do We Need the Church?* (New York, 1969), 112.

15. Quoted in David P. Gaines, *The World Council of Churches: A Study of Its Background and History* (Peterborough, N.H., 1966), 430.

16. For a survey of integralism in twentieth-century American Catholicism, see Philip Gleason's presidential address to the Ameri-

can Catholic Historical Association, "In Search of Unity: American Catholic Thought 1920–1960," *Catholic Historical Review* LXV (1979), 185–205.

17. Quotations from typescripts of speeches in the Archives of the Boston Archdiocese.

18. The statement on interfaith meetings, a favorite at St. Benedict Center, appears, among other places, in Catherine G. Clarke, "The Failure of Inter-Faith" *From the Housetops* I, no. 2 (December, 1946), 46. All other quotations come from interviews with Feeney conducted by Ben Bagdikian in the *Providence Evening Bulletin*, April 20 and May 23, 1949.

19. Clarke, *The Loyolas and the Cabots*, 96–97.

CHAPTER 5

1. Walter Johnson, ed., *The Papers of Adlai E. Stevenson*, Vol. IV (Boston, 1974), 128.

2. *New York Times*, September 8, 1947; on the Catholic press, see Alfred McClung Lee, "The Press and Public Relations of Religious Bodies," *Annals of the American Academy of Political and Social Science* 256 (1948), 129; *Public Opinion Quarterly* 11 (1947–48), 643; and 13 (1949–50), 712.

3. Ralph Lord Roy, *Communism and the Churches* (New York, 1960), 232–35, 254–60.

4. J. B. Matthews, "Reds and Our Churches," *American Mercury*, July, 1953, 13.

5. *New York Times*, July 10, 1953; for accounts of the Matthews affair, see Roy, *op. cit.*, 248–53, and Donald F. Crosby, *God, Church, and Flag: Senator Joseph P. McCarthy and the Catholic Church, 1950–1957* (Chapel Hill, N.C., 1978), 126–30.

6. Paul Hutchinson, *The New Leviathan* (Chicago, 1946), 10; *Partisan Review* 17 (1950), 103, 231; Arthur Schlesinger, Jr., *The Vital Center* (Boston, 1949), 1, 10.

7. John Foster Dulles, *War or Peace* (New York, 1950), 251–56; Will Herberg "Prophetic Faith in an Age of Crisis," *Judaism* 1 (1952), 199, 198.

8. Walter Millis, ed., *The Forrestal Diaries* (New York, 1951), 128; Fulton J. Sheen, *Communism and the Conscience of the West* (Indianapolis, 1948), 76–77; William Hordern, *Christianity, Communism and History* (New York–Nashville, 1954), 54–55.

9. Louis Francis Budenz, *This Is My Story* (New York, 1947), 166; *Time*, November 29, 1948, 46.

10. Whittaker Chambers, *Witness* (New York, 1952), 9, 12, 16–17, 449.

11. Reinhold Niebuhr, *The Irony of American History* (New York, 1952), 15; J. Paul Williams, *What Americans Believe and How They Worship* (New York, 1952), 367–74.

12. *Christian Century* 69 (April 3, 1952), 1000–1001; *Partisan Review* 17 (1950), 607–9.

13. Roper polls quoted in Will Herberg, *Protestant Catholic Jew* (rev. ed. New York, 1960), 51; *A Man Called Peter* (New York, 1951), 232.

14. Quoted in the *Congressional Record* (1954), 7763. The Pledge had been made more definitive once before. Composed at the end of the nineteenth century (in the form of "I pledge allegiance to my flag, and to the republic for which it stands. . ."), and published in *The Youth's Companion* magazine as part of a campaign to place an American flag in every American schoolroom, it was amended after World War I to include the words "of the United States of America"—lest immigrant schoolchildren have any doubt about which country they were pledging their allegiance to.

15. *New York Times*, May 5, 1954.

16. *Congressional Record*, 1954, 8618.

17. *Ibid.*, 1600, 607B, 7763, 7758; *New York Times*, May 17, 1954.

18. *Congressional Record*, 1952, A911; Dulles, *op. cit.*, 259–61; *Congressional Record*, 1954, 7758.

19. *Congressional Record*, 1954, 7764; 1955, 7533.

20. Herberg, *op. cit.*, 271.

21. *Christianity and Crisis* XVI (March 5, 1956), 18.

22. *Ibid.* (April 2, 1956), 40.

23. *Christian Century* 73 (1956), 640–42, 848–49, 921–22, 1197–99.

24. *Christian Century* 72 (1955), 1076.

25. "Report of the General Board's Commission to Study Evangelism," Document of Record #505 (1957), in possession of National Council of Churches, New York, N.Y.; *The Good News of God: The Nature and Task of Evangelism*" (New York, 1957), 20; "Report by the Executive Director to the Board of Managers of the Central Department of Evangelism" (May 8, 1957), Archives of the National Council of Churches (NCA).

26. *Life* 43 (July 1, 1957), 87, 92; see *Christian Century* 74 (1957), 677–78, 749–51, 933–34.

27. Noel Houston, "Billy Graham," *Holiday* (February, 1958); letter in NCA.

28. *Life* 44 (June 9, 1958), 122; for Van Dusen's account of his Caribbean holiday, see *The Christian Century* 72 (1955), 946–48; for NAE membership at the time, see *Christianity Today* 9 (1958) [425]; Martin Marty, *The New Shape of American Religion* (New York, 1959), 21, 89.

29. Reinhold Niebuhr, *Pious and Secular America* (New York, 1958), 51, 108.

CHAPTER 6

1. The story was covered closely by *The Christian Century*; for the chronology of events I have relied most on "The Lawson-Vanderbilt Story" (March 23, 341–42), "Sit-Ins Prod a Community" (March 30, 379–82), and "Vanderbilt's Time of Testing" (August 10, 921–25).

2. *Christian Century* 77, April 13, 1960, 444, 454.

3. *Christian Century* 77, August 10, 1960, 925.

4. Martin Luther King, Jr., *Why We Can't Wait* (New York, 1964), 61, 59.

5. *Christianity in Crisis* (December 28, 1959), 192.

6. Martin Luther King, Jr., "Pilgrimage to Nonviolence," *Christian Century* 77, March 13, 1960, 41.

7. Gibson Winter, *The Suburban Captivity of the Church* (Garden City, N.Y., 1961), 163, 166, 162.

8. Theodore Sorensen, *Kennedy* (New York, 1965), 209.

9. For Spellman and the 1960 election see John Cooney, *The American Pope: The Life and Times of Francis Cardinal Spellman* (New York, 1984), 268–72.

10. *Look*, March 3, 1959, 17; *America* 100 (March 7, 1959), 651; quotation from the *St. Louis Review* taken from a roundup of Catholic press opinion on the Kennedy comment in *Commonweal* 69 (March 20, 1959), 648.

11. Quoted in Lawrence H. Fuchs, *John F. Kennedy and American Catholicism* (New York, 1967), 168.

12. Sorensen, *op. cit*, 144.

13. "A Protestant View of a Catholic for President," *Look*, May 10, 1960, 31–34.

14. See, for example, John A. Ryan and Moorhouse F. X. Millar, *The State and the Church* (New York, 1924), 29*ff*.

15. Sorensen, *op. cit.*, 190.

16. Sorensen, *op. cit.*, 188.

17. Sorensen, *op. cit.*, 191.

18. Mathew Ahmann, ed., *Race: Challenge to Religion* (Chicago, 1963), v.

19. Ahmann, *op. cit.*, 133–34; Balfour Brickner, "Notes on the National Conference on Religion and Race," mimeograph in The Jewish Labor Committee—Michigan Region Collection of the Archives of Labor History and Urban Affairs, University Archives, Wayne State University.

20. Ahmann, *op. cit.*, 171, 173, 91, 6.

21. *Christianity in Crisis*, May 29, 1961, 99.

22. James Baldwin, *The Fire Next Time* (New York, 1985), 84, 82.

23. *Ibid.*, 113, 129.

24. William Stringfellow, *My People Is the Enemy* (New York, 1964), 139; *New York Times*, August 30, 1963.

25. Martin Luther King, Jr., *Why We Can't Wait*, 96–100.

26. Walker Percy, "Stoicism in the South," *Commonweal* 64 (1956), 343–44.

27. Walker Percy, "The Failure and the Hope," in Will D. Campbell and James Y. Holloway, eds., *The Failure and the Hope* (Grand Rapids, 1972), 25, 28, 17.

28. Garry Wills, *Bare Ruined Choirs* (Garden City, N.Y., 1972), 94.

29. Harvey Cox, *The Secular City: Secularization and Urbanization in Theological Perspective* (New York, 1965), 242.

CHAPTER 7

1. Diane Kennedy Pike, *Search: The Personal Story of a Wilderness Journey* (Garden City, N.Y., 1970), 177; Joan Didion, "James Pike, American," in *The White Album* (New York, 1979), 57; William Stringfellow and Anthony Towne, *The Death and Life of Bishop Pike* (Garden City, N.Y., 1976), 41.

2. Stringfellow and Towne, *op. cit.*, 312.

3. William Stringfellow and Anthony Towne, *The Bishop Pike Affair* (New York, 1967), 25.

4. Robert Gordis, *Judaism in a Christian World* (New York, 1966), 154–55.

5. Arthur A. Cohen, *The Myth of the Judeo-Christian Tradition* (New York, 1970), xv–xviii, 199. Cohen offered no support for his claims about the German Higher Critics and the Judeo-Christian tradition. The passage in question is worth quoting at length: "It was only in the late nineteenth century in Germany that the Judeo-Christian tradition, as such, was first defined. It was introduced by German Protestant scholarship to account for the findings developed by the Higher Criticism of the Old Testament and achieved considerable

currency as a polemical term in that period. There quite clearly, the negative significance of the expression became primary. The emphasis fell not to the communality of the word 'tradition' but to the accented stress of the hyphen. The Jewish was latinized and abbreviated into 'Judeo' to indicate a dimension, albeit a pivotal dimension, of the explicit Christian experience." Precisely what term did the German scholars introduce? The latinized "Judeo-" occurs in English and French but not in German, which permits no invidious distinction between the two hyphenated adjectives by using "jüdisch-christlich" for "Judeo-Christian." The Higher Critics were deeply concerned with the Jewish sources of Christianity, but I can find no polemicizing over a "jüdisch-christliche Uberlieferung" as such.

6. Ibid., 201, xii, 200, 217, 222. For a more detailed discussion of Cohen's case, see my "Notes on the Judeo-Christian Tradition in America," American Quarterly (Spring, 1984), 80–82.

7. Walter Arnold, Commonweal 96 (April 2, 1970), 96–97; Jacob Neusner, "Beyond Accommodation," Midstream 16 (March, 1970), 77–78; John Osterreicher, America 122 (June 6, 1970), 617.

8. For a survey of American reaction to the Six-Day War, see Lucy S. Dawidowicz, "American Public Opinion," American Jewish Yearbook 1968–69, 198–229 (unless otherwise indicated, all quotations on the war come from this source); New York Times, June 23, 1967; June 27, 1967.

9. New York Times, July 7, 1967; Christian Century 84 (1967), 883–84.

10. Interchurch News (August-September, 1967), 4; Christian Century 84 (1967), 84–85.

11. Eliezer Berkovitz, "Judaism in the Post-Christian Era," Judaism 15 (1966), 80, 223, 16, 363; "Christians and the Mideast Crisis," Christian Century 84 (1967), 963.

12. Nathan Rotenstreich, "Emancipation and Its Aftermath," in David Sidorsky, ed., The Future of the Jewish Community in America (New York, 1973), 52.

13. David Polish, "Why American Jews Are Disillusioned," Christian Century 84 (1967), 966. For the other point of view see Milton Himmelfarb, "In Light of Israel's Victory," Commentary 44 (October, 1967), 53–61, and Richard Rubenstein, "Did Christians Fail Israel?," Commonweal 87 (1967), 297–98.

14. Christian Century 84 (1967), 883.

15. Robert N. Bellah, "Civil Religion in America," in Religion in America, William G. McLoughlin and Robert N. Bellah, eds. (Boston, 1968), 3–23.

16. New York Times, November 29, 1965; on the responsibility

for Daniel Berrigan's trip to Latin America, see James Hennessey, *American Catholics: A History of the Roman Catholic Community in the United States* (New York, 1981), 319.

17. Francine du Plessix Gray, *Divine Disobedience: Profiles in Catholic Radicalism* (New York, 1971), 124–25, 77, 175, 189, 199; William Stringfellow and Anthony Towne, *Suspect Tenderness: The Ethics of the Berrigan Witness* (New York, 1971), 22.

18. *Ibid.*, 60, 24.

19. Mitchell Goodman, *The Movement Toward a New America* (New York–Philadelphia, 1970), 627–56.

20. Gray, *op, cit.*, 120; Stan Iverson, "Sex and Anarcho-Socialism," *Appeal to Reason* (Seattle), II (March, 1966), 2–3 (quoted in Laurence Veysey, *The Communal Experience: Anarchist and Mystical Communities in Twentieth-Century America* (Chicago, 2nd ed., 1978), 434; Gary Snyder, *Earth House Hold* (New York, 1969), 92.

21. Carlos Castaneda, *The Teachings of Don Juan* (Berkeley, 1968), 125.

22. William James, *The Will to Believe* (New York, 1956), 319; on the unmasking of Castaneda, see Richard De Mille, *The Don Juan Papers: Further Castaneda Controversies* (Santa Barbara, 1980). If drugs were central to the enterprise in *The Teachings*, Castaneda's subsequent works, always attuned to the ideological moment, moved on to natural highs and even feminism.

CHAPTER 8

1. *New York Times*, September 18, 1980.

2. *Richmond Times-Dispatch*, October 2, 1980; *New York Times*, October 10, 1980; *Washington Post*, October 4, 1980.

3. Frances FitzGerald, *Cities on a Hill* (New York, 1986), 121–201.

4. Jerry Falwell, *Listen, America!* (Garden City, N.Y., 1980), 28, 244, 255, 266.

5. *New York Times*, October 11, 1980.

6. *New York Times*, October 7, 1986.

7. *New York Times*, December 19, 1980; April 22, 1981; June 11, 1981; Baptist Press Service, June 25, 1987.

8. *New York Times*, November 23, 1980.

9. *New York Times*, November 26, 1980; December 9, 1980.

10. Nathan Perlmutter and Ruth Ann Perlmutter, *The Real Anti-Semitism in America* (New York, 1982), 154, 156, 172.

11. Dean R. Hoge and David A. Roozen, *Understanding Church Growth and Decline: 1950–1978* (New York–Philadelphia, 1979), 333; see William Hutchison, "Past Imperfect: History and the Pros-

pect for Liberalism," in Robert S. Michaelson and Wade Clark Roof, *Liberal Protestantism: Realities and Possibilities* (New York, 1986), 65–82.

12. Harvey Cox, *Religion in the Secular City* (New York, 1984), 267.

13. *Moral Majority Report* (May, 1983), 8.

14. Slip opinion of Judge W. Brevard Hand in *Smith* v. *Board of School Commissioners of Mobile County*, United States District Court for the Southern District of Alabama, Southern Division. The decision was subsequently overturned by the U.S. Circuit Court of Appeals.

15. Richard John Neuhaus, *The Naked Public Square* (Grand Rapids, 1984), 164, 110, 146, 37, 23.

16. Robert N. Bellah, *The Broken Covenant: American Civil Religion in Time of Trial* (New York, 1975), 142; Robert N. Bellah et al., *Habits of the Heart: Individualism and Commitment in American Life* (New York, 1985), 246, 239, 221, 235.

17. William James, *The Varieties of Religious Experience* (Cambridge, 1985), 413.

18. Werner Sollors, *Beyond Ethnicity: Consent and Descent in American Culture* (New York, 1986), 190.

19. Christopher Lasch, *The Culture of Narcissism: American Life in an Age of Diminishing Expectation* (New York, 1979), 21.

20. David Roozen, William McKinney, and Wayne Thompson, "The Big Chill Warms to Worship: Family Cycle and Political Orientation Effects on Increases in Worship Attendance from the 1970's to 1980's among the Baby Boom Generation," paper presented at SSSR/ RRA Annual Meeting, November 16, 1986.

21. Rosemary Radford Ruether, *Disputed Questions: On Being a Christian* (Nashville, 1982), 43–56; Michael Harrington, *The Politics at God's Funeral* (New York, 1983), 6; *Christian Century* 103 (October 8, 1986), 859; Wade Clark Roof and William McKinney, *American Mainline Religion: Its Changing Shape and Future* (New Brunswick, N.J., 1987), 17; *New York Times*, April 19, 1987.

22. John Murray Cuddihy, *The Ordeal of Civility* (New York, 1974), 231.

■ INDEX

Abrams, Roy, 22
adhesion, 19–21, 39, 53, 107, 150
  anti-Catholicism and, 122–23
  anti-Communism and, 87, 94,
    100–101
  Graham and, 64, 68–69
  see also Judeo-Christian
    tradition
Agee, James, 30–31
Age of Anxiety, The (Auden), 32
Ahmann, Mathew, 126
Allen, Jimmy, 164–65
Aslop, Joseph, 32–33
Alsop, Stewart, 32–33
Altizer, Thomas, 133
America (Jesuit weekly), 52–53,
  71, 90, 119–20
American Century, 64
American Council of Christian
  Churches (ACCC), 58–60
American Freedom and Catholic
  Power (Blanshard), 123
American Institute of Public
  Opinion, 33
American jeremiad, 66, 67, 68,
  158, 164
Americanism, 85–86, 122

American Jewish Committee (AJC),
  160
American religion, 15–22
  consensus in, 16–17
  Emerson's views on, 16–17
  polls on, 17
  Protestantism as, 16–17, 20–22
  skin-deep quality of, 17–18
  statistics on, 17, 38–39, 179
American Revolution, 20
Anti-Defamation League (ADL),
  166, 168
anti-Semitism, 41–42, 73, 77, 79,
  82, 160–62, 167–69
antiwar movement, 140, 148–54
anxiety, 91
  atomic bomb and, 32–35, 64–65
  Graham crusades and, 64–65,
    73–74
  religious conversion and, 37–38
  St. Benedict Center and, 73–74
Aquinas, Saint Thomas, 26–27, 80
Arian controversy, 81
Arminianism, 66–67, 178
Army, U.S., 97
Arnold, Matthew, 46
Asch, Sholem, 38

atomic bomb, 23–37, 64–65
    anxiety and, 32–35, 64–65
    Apocalypse compared to, 27
    inner peace and, 33–35
    polls on, 27, 33
    religious views on, 23–29, 36–
        37
    scientific views on, 29–31
Auden, W. H., 31, 32

Baldwin, James, 128–29
Baptists, 60–61, 160–71
Barth, Karl, 45
Barton, Bruce, 21
Baruch, Bernard, 56, 57
Begin, Menachem, 168
Bellah, Robert, 149–50, 175–76
Bellarmine, Robert, 71
Bennett, John, 25, 46, 61–62, 114,
    115, 116
Bentley, Elizabeth, 93
Berger, Peter, 100–101
Bergstrom, Charles V., 165
Berkovitz, Eliezer, 146
Berrigan, Daniel, 140, 149–54
Berrigan, Philip, 140, 150, 154
Beyond God the Father (Daly), 158
Bible, 17, 45, 62, 94
Bigart, Homer, 149
Black Muslims, 128–29, 146
Blackmur, R. P., 31
Blake, Eugene Carson, 121, 139
Blanshard, Paul, 123
Bolton, Oliver, 99
Bonhoeffer, Dietrich, 133–34
Bonnell, Rev. John Sutherland, 90
Boston College, 80–81, 83
Boston Heresy Case, 81, 86
Boulding, Kenneth, 19
Brandeis University, 82
Branscomb, Harvie, 109–14
Brickner, Balfour, 126, 144
Bridge, The (yearbook of the
    Institute of Judaeo-Christian
    Studies), 52
Briskman, Mark, 166
Brooks, Overton, 98–99
Brown, Norman O., 154
Brown, Robert McAfee, 120
Brunner, Emil, 45
Bryson, Lyman, 42
Budenz, Louis, 93

Bulletin of the Atomic Scientists,
    29
Bunyan, John, 36
Burnstein, Alexander J., 50–51
Burnt-Over District, 17
Bush, Douglas, 42
Bushnell, Horace, 50

Calhoun, Robert L., 25, 104
Carnegie, Dale, 34, 35
Carnell, E. J., 103
Carter, Jimmy, 166
Castaneda, Carlos, 155–56, 157
Catholics, see Roman Catholicism,
    Roman Catholics
"Catholics and Communism"
    (Cushing), 77
Catholic World, 26, 30
Challenge of Israel's Faith, The
    (Wright), 45
Chambers, Whittaker, 93
Chavez, Caesar, 140
Chesterton, G. K., 71
"Christian Amendment," 100
"Christian Americanization," 21
Christian Century, 24, 58, 60–61,
    95, 102, 103, 105, 110–15,
    139, 145–46, 148, 180
Christianity:
    as conversion religion, 19–20
    Third Force in, 106–7
    see also Judeo-Christian
        tradition; specific sects
Christianity, Communism and
    History (Hordern), 92
Christianity and Crisis, 101, 114
Christianity and Social Progress
    (Rauschenbusch), 115–16
Christianity and the Children of
    Israel (Eckardt), 47–48
Christian Looks at the Jewish
    Question, A (Maritain), 41–42
Christian Science, 35
Church of England, 16
"Civil Religion in America"
    (Bellah), 149–50
civil rights, 108–16, 125–32, 138,
    140, 148, 150, 168
Clarke, Catherine, 71–74, 83
Clergy and Laymen Concerned
    About Vietnam, 148–51
Cohen, Arthur A., 142–44

cold war, religious dimension of,
    87–99, 107
Commentary, 143
Commission on the Relation of the
    Church to the War in the Light
    of the Christian Faith
    (Calhoun Commission), 24–25
Commonweal, 143
Communism, 35, 44, 65, 85, 87–
    99, 171
    as religion, 92–93, 94, 99
Communism and the Conscience
    of the West (Sheen), 92
Conant, James Bryant, 74
Conference of Southern Baptist
    Evangelists, 167
Conference on Science, Philosophy
    and Religion in Their Relation
    to the Democratic Way of Life,
    Inc., 42, 43, 44, 46
Congress, U.S., 95–100, 147
    see also House of
    Representatives, U.S.
Constitution, U.S., 21, 99–100,
    119–20, 122, 124, 172, 173
    "Christian Amendment" and,
    100
    First Amendment of, 18, 52, 174
conversion religions, 19–20, 49,
    53–86, 163
    Graham and, 54–69
    Roman Catholicism and, 26, 36,
    37–38, 71, 73, 74, 84–85, 93,
    107
Coolidge, Julian Lowell, 70
Costain, Thomas, 38
Coughlin, Father, 41
Cox, Harvey, 134–35, 155, 171
Cronkite, Walter, 98
Cuddihy, John Murray, 181
Culture and Anarchy (Arnold),
    46
Cushing, Richard J., 26, 70, 73, 76–
    79, 81, 82, 83, 85, 119

Dahlberg, Edwin, 106
Daly, Mary, 158
Darwinian evolution, 15, 21
Davis, James P., 117, 118
Day, Dorothy, 26, 71, 148
Death of God theologians, 133–34,
    135, 139

"Dedication Day" (Agee), 30–31,
    32
democracy, 19, 20, 91, 175
    anti-Communism and, 91–92,
    94–99
    Judeo-Christian tradition and,
    40–44, 50, 120
Depression, Great, 21–22
DeVries, Peter, 53
Dewey, John, 31, 32, 43
Didion, Joan, 137
dispensational premillennialism,
    157–58
Docherty, Rev. George M., 96, 97,
    98
Donnelly, Philip J., 80, 81
Donovan, Hedley, 57
drugs, 155–56
Dulles, Avery, 71, 72–73, 74
Dulles, John Foster, 23, 24, 91–92,
    99
Dunn, James, 161

Eckardt, A. Roy, 47–48, 100
ecumenism, 57, 58, 60, 69, 77, 84,
    90, 126, 139, 140, 148, 164–
    165, 172, 175, 177
Eddy, Mary Baker, 35
Edwards, Jonathan, 50
Egan, John J., 127
Eighteenth Amendment, 21
Eisendrath, Maurice, 90
Eisenhower, Dwight D., 40, 44, 68,
    90, 96, 98, 119, 138
Eisenhower, Mamie, 96
Eliot, T. S., 38
Emerson, Ralph Waldo, 13, 16–17,
    177
Episcopalianism, 136–41, 163
Espy, R. H. Edwin, 145–46
ethnicity, 177–78
evangelical Protestantism, 15, 39,
    54–69, 115, 157–58
    Niebuhr vs. 101–7
    in U.S. history, 16–17, 20–21
    see also fundamentalism
extra ecclesiam nulla salus,
    doctrine of, 75, 80, 81, 84
Eyes of Faith (Minear), 45

Falwell, Jerry, 159, 162–65, 167–
    169, 172, 179

Farris, Berlyn, 62–63, 103–4
fascism, opposition to, 41–44
FCC, see Federal Council of
    Churches
Feast of Fools, The (Cox), 171
Federal Council of Churches
    (FCC), 21, 23–25, 27, 58–60,
    120
Feeney, Leonard, 71–76, 78–86
    anti-Semitism of, 73, 82
    dismissed from Society of Jesus,
      82
    silencing of, 81
Feeneyites, 81–83, 86
Fellowship of Reconciliation, 109
feminism, 158
Ferguson, Horace, 97, 98
Ferré, Nels, 46
Finkelstein, Louis, 42
Finney, Charles G., 66
First Amendment, 18, 52, 174
FitzGerald, Frances, 163
Flanders, Ralph, 99–100
Forrestal, James, 92
Foundation for Religious
    Transition, The, 137, 141,
    155
Fourth Great Awakening, 39, 53,
    100–101
    see also Judeo-Christian
      tradition
Frank, Waldo, 48
freedom, 18, 52, 94, 174
    religious, 20, 97, 161
Freeman, Joseph, 41
French Revolution, 65
Friedrich, Carl, 41
From the Housetops (St. Benedict
    Center magazine), 73, 74, 77,
    80, 81
fundamentalism, 15, 21–22, 55,
    57–62, 63–64, 157, 159
    see also evangelical
      Protestantism; Moral Majority

Gallup, George, 27, 33
Gallup Poll, 27, 33, 88, 147
Gandhi, Mahatma, 116
Germany, Lutheranism in, 17–18
Gettysburg Address, 96
Gilkey, Langdon, 116
Ginsberg, Allen, 154, 155

God in Search of Man (Heschel),
    49
God That Failed, The, 93
Goodman, Mitchell, 153
Gordis, David, 180–81
Gordis, Robert, 50, 142
Graham, Billy (William Franklin
    Graham, Jr.), 54–69, 115, 119,
    157–58, 161, 171
    on atomic bomb, 64–65, 73–74
    Bennett's views on, 61–62
    Niebuhr vs., 101–7
    political views of, 64
    sermons of, 64–68, 99
Great Awakenings, 16, 20, 21, 39
Great Britain, 16, 65
Guareschi, Giovanni, 38
Guide to Confident Living, A
    (Peale), 34

Habits of the Heart (Bellah), 175
Hamilton, William, 133
Hand, W. Brevard, 172, 173, 178
Harkness, Georgia, 103
Harrington, Michael, 180
Harvard College, 70–71, 73–79
Hearst, William Randolph, 55, 57
Hebraism:
    Hellenism vs., 45–46, 49, 51
    see also Judeo-Christian
      tradition
Hellenism vs. Hebraism, 45–46,
    49, 51
Heller, Bernard, 51
Henry, Carl, 59
Herberg, Will, 17–18, 49–50, 92,
    101, 134, 177
Heschel, Abraham, 48–49, 127,
    149–52
Higgins, George G., 145, 165
High Table, 70, 78
Hiss, Alger, 93–94, 119
Hofmann, Paul, 118
Hoge, Dean R., 170–71
Holmes, John Haynes, 24, 34
Homrighausen, E. G., 102–3
Honest to God (Robinson), 139
Hook, Sidney, 31, 43, 91
Hordern, William, 92
"Hour of Decision" (radio
    program), 68
House of Representatives, U.S., 97

Un-American Activities
Committee of, 88–90
Houston, Noel, 105
Howland, William, 56
How to Stop Worrying and Start
Living (Carnegie), 34
Hughes, Emmett John, 90
Human Destiny (Noüy), 35
Humani Generis, 83–84
Humphrey, Hubert, 122
Hutchins, Robert, 73
Hutchinson, Paul, 91

immigration, 20, 21
individualism, 67, 175, 178
inner peace:
religious conversion and, 37–38
self-help and, 33–35, 138
Institute of Judaeo-Christian
Studies, 52–53, 143–44
Israel, 144–47, 158, 164, 166–
169
"Is There a Judeo-Christian
Tradition?" (Tillich), 47

Jackson, Donald, 88–89
James, William, 13, 156, 176–77
Janney, Russell, 38
Japan, in World War II, 23–31, 36,
73–74
Jehovah's Witnesses, 22, 170
Jesuits, 52–53, 71–76, 78–83
John XXIII, Pope, 52
Judaism, 146
Judaism, Jews, 16, 20, 90, 100, 107,
160–69, 179
Anti-Semitism and, 41–42, 73,
77, 79, 82, 160–62, 167–69
as exclusive religion, 19
see also Judeo-Christian
tradition; specific groups
"Judaism and Christianity"
(Herberg), 49–50
Judaism and Modern Man
(Herberg), 49
Judeo-Christian Institute, 52–53,
143–44
Judeo-Christian tradition, 40–53,
69, 120, 125, 131, 150, 154
American jeremiad and, 66
Communism and, 89, 94, 100–
101, 107

opposition to fascism and, 41–
44
opposition to idea of, 43–44, 50–
52, 142–48
original meaning of, 40–41
theological dimension of, 44–50
traditional values and, 172–75
just-war theory, 26–27

Kazin, Alfred, 48
Kelley, Dean, 170
Kennedy, John F., 118–25
Kennedy, Joseph, 119
Kennedy, Robert F., 76, 137
Kennedy, Scott, 141
Kierkegaard, Søren, 32
King, Martin Luther, Jr., 112–16,
125, 127 32, 140, 148
Knox, Ronald, 79
Krock, Arthur, 118
Kushner, Harold, 179

Langer, William, 100
LaPorte, Roger, 148, 150
Larson, Sheila, 176
Lasch, Christopher, 178
Late Great Planet Earth, The
(Lindsey), 157–58, 164
Lawson, James M., Jr., 108–14, 116
"Letter from a Region of My Mind"
(Baldwin), 128–29
"Letter from Birmingham Jail"
(King), 131
Levovitz, Pesach Z., 144–45
liberalism, 115, 138, 150, 168–69,
170
anti-Communism and, 87, 91, 94
Catholic criticism of, 71–75
Liebman, Joshua Loth, 33–34, 35,
179
Life magazine, 105, 106
Lincoln, Abraham, 95, 96
Lincoln, Eric, 128
Lindeman, Eduard C., 28
Lindsey, Hal, 157–58
Lippmann, Walter, 92
Listen, America! (Falwell), 164
Look magazine, 119–22, 137
Lowell House, 70, 78–79
Luce, Clare Boothe, 36–37, 56, 71,
79
Luce, Henry, 26–27, 56–57, 64

Lutheranism, in Post-Reformation Germany, 17–18

McCall's magazine, 36–37
McCarthy, Joseph, 89–90, 97
McConnell, H. H., 103, 106
McCormick, Vincent, 80–81
Macdonald, Dwight, 28–31
McEleney, John J., 79, 80
Machen, J. Gresham, 58–59
McIntire, Carl, 58–59
McKinney, William, 180
McKnight, H. J., 60
McLoughlin, William, 57, 68
McManus, James E., 117–18
Malcolm X, 128, 129
Maluf, Fakhri, 80
Man Called Peter, A (C. Marshall), 96
Man Nobody Knows, The (Barton), 21
Mao Zedong, 86
March on Washington, 129–31, 148
Maritain, Jacques, 31, 41–42, 52
Maritain, Raïssa, 42
Marshall, Catherine, 95–96
Marshall, Peter, 95–96
Martínez, Luis Aponte, 117, 118
Marty, Martin, 100, 107, 120, 175, 180
Marxist Progressivism, 29
Massachusetts Committee of Catholics, Protestants, and Jews, 77
materialism, 99
Matthews, J. B., 89–90
Mauldin, Bill, 93
Mayer, Milton, 29–30
Mays, Benjamin E., 127
Mead, Sidney, 18–19
Mehta, Ved, 133
Meiklejohn, Alexander, 73
Mencken, H. L., 21
Merton, Thomas, 37–38
Mexican-American war, 149–50
Meyer, Cardinal, 126
Midstream, 143
Miller, J. Kenneth, 60
Mind Cure (positive thinking), 34, 35
Mindszenty, Cardinal, 88

Minear, Paul, 45
Mississippi Summer Project (1964), 132
"Mist of Death over New York" (Parker), 33
Moody, Dwight L., 66
Moody Bible Institute, 27
"Morality for the Atomic Age" (Lindeman), 28
Moral Majority, 162–65, 167–69, 172, 175, 179
Morgan, Temple, 76, 78
Morgenstern, Julian, 43
Mormonism, 20
Movement Toward a New America, The, 153–55
Moyers, Bill, 167
Muhammad, Elijah, 128–29
Mumford, Lewis, 28, 29
Muñoz Marín, Luis, 117–18
Murch, James DeForest, 60
Murphy, Arthur E., 44
Murphy, Francis X., 30
Murray, John Courtney, 26, 51–52, 123
Muste, A. J., 24, 27, 109
My People Is the Enemy (Stringfellow), 130
Mystici Corporis (Pius XII), 83–84
Myth of the Judeo-Christian Tradition, The (Cohen), 142–144

NAE, see National Association of Evangelicals for United Action
Nagel, Ernest, 43
Naked Public Square, The (Neuhaus), 174–75
Nashville Banner, 109
Nasser, Gamal Abdel, 144, 145
National Affairs Briefing, 159–61, 167, 168
National Association of Evangelicals for United Action (NAE), 58–60, 106, 158
National Catholic Welfare Conference, 125–26
National Conference of Christians and Jews (NCCJ), 90, 126
National Conference of Citizens for Religious Freedom, 123

National Conference on Race and
Religion (1963), 126–29
National Council of Churches
(NCC), 58–64, 102–4, 125–26,
132, 139, 145, 151, 169, 170
national religion:
Emerson's views on, 13, 16–17
see also American religion
Nation of Islam, see Black
Muslims
NCC, see National Council of
Churches
Nelson, J. Robert, 109, 112, 113
New Evangelicalism, 58–69
Neuhaus, Richard, 149–52, 174–
75
Neusner, Jacob, 143, 146
"New Failure of Nerve, The"
(Partisan Review symposium),
30, 31
New Shape of American Religion,
The (Marty), 100, 107
New Yorker magazine, 128–29,
133, 163
New York Herald Tribune, 34
New York Times, 133, 136, 145,
149, 165–66, 168
Next Day, The (Pike), 138, 141
Niebuhr, Reinhold, 25, 32, 45–47,
49, 50–51, 94, 115, 138, 148
Graham vs., 101–7
Niebuhrians, 116–17
Nietzsche, Friedrich, 133
Nixon, Richard M., 119, 171
Nock, Arthur Darby, 19
nonviolence, 108–16
Noüy, Pierre Lecompte du, 35

O'Brien, Monsignor John A., 90
Ockenga, Rev. Harold, 56
O'Connell, William Cardinal, 70,
77
Oesterreicher, John M., 52, 143–
44
"Open Letter," of Protestant
leaders (May 1960), 121, 122
Ordeal of Civility, The (Cuddihy),
181
Orwell, George, 32, 41
Osservatore Romano, 25, 118
Other Side, The (Pike and Pike),
140

Oxnam, G. Bromley, 23, 24, 88–89,
120–22
Oxtoby, Willard G., 146

pacifism, 22, 24–25
Palestine Liberation Organization
(PLO), 169
Parker, David, 33
parochial schools, federal aid to,
119, 121
Partisan Review, 30, 31, 38, 43, 48,
52, 91 ·
Peace of Mind (Liebman), 33–34,
37, 179
Peace of Soul (Sheen), 37
Peale, Norman Vincent, 34, 35,
103, 105, 123, 179
Pekin Daily Times, 27
Percy, Walker, 131–32, 135
Perkins, Elliott, 70, 78
Perlmutter, Nathan, 166, 168–69,
172
Perlmutter, Ruth Ann, 168–69,
172
Phillips, William, 38
Pike, Diane Kennedy, 136, 137,
140, 141
Pike, James, Jr., 140
Pike, James Albert, Sr., 136–42,
152, 153, 155
Pilgrim's Progress (Bunyan), 36
Pius IX, Pope, 75
Pius X, Pope, 79
Pius XII, Pope, 68, 83
Pledge of Allegiance, 96–99
Poling, Daniel, 44
Polish, David, 148
Politics (journal), 28–31
Pope, Lister, 111
positive thinking (Mind Cure), 34,
35
Preachers Present Arms (Abrams),
22
Presbyterianism, 58–60, 68, 95–96,
97
Program for Survival, 28
progress, decline of faith in, 31–32
Prohibition, 21
"Proposal to Billy Graham"
(Niebuhr), 103
"Proposal to Reinhold Niebuhr, A"
(Carnell), 103

Protestant Catholic Jew (Herberg), 50, 101, 134, 177
Protestant Digest, 41
Protestantism, Protestants, 84, 86, 142–43
  as American religion, 16–17, 20–22
  anti-Communism and, 88–91
  atomic bomb as viewed by, 23–25
  evangelical, *see* evangelical Protestantism
  Judeo-Christian tradition and, 44–46, 51–52
  Kennedy candidacy and, 121–24
  see also specific sects and organizations
Protestant Reformation, 16, 46
Protestants and Other Americans United for the Separation of Church and State, 120–21
Protestants Answer Anti-Semitism (handbook), 41
"Protestant View of a Catholic for President, A" 121–22
psychotherapy, 35
Puerto Rico, 117–18
Puritans, 66

Rabaut, Louis, 97–98, 100
Rauschenbusch, Walter, 115–16
Reader's Digest, 33
Reagan, Ronald, 160, 162–63, 164, 166, 168
Real Anti-Semitism in America, The (Perlmutter and Perlmutter), 168–69
"Reds and Our Churches" (Matthews), 89
Reformed Church in America, 59
religion:
  exclusive vs. inclusive, 19–20
  science vs., 15, 21, 31, 35
  see also specific topics
"Religion" (Emerson), 16–17
"Religion and the Intellectuals" (*Partisan Review* symposium), 31, 38, 48, 91
religious pluralism, 44, 165–66, 178
  in Roman Empire, 19–20
Religious Roundtable, 159–60

religious toleration, 15, 19–20, 77
religious tribalism, 175–76
Reston, James, 130
revivals, *see* evangelical Protestantism
Rieff, Philip, 178
Riesman, David, 31
Rivers, L. Mendel, 147
Robertson, Pat, 159, 179
Robinson, Henry Morton, 38
Robinson, John, 139
Rockefeller, John D., III, 111
Rodino, Peter, 100
"Role of Religion in American Destiny, The" (Williams), 94–95
Roman Catholicism, Roman Catholics, 15, 16, 36–38, 71–86, 96–97, 117–26, 143, 160, 161, 169
  Americanism and, 85–86
  anti-Communism and, 88–90
  atomic bomb as viewed by, 25–26, 36–37, 73–74
  conversions to, 26, 36, 37–38, 71, 73, 74, 84–85, 93, 107
  democracy and, 20
  Judeo-Christian heritage as viewed by, 41–42, 51–53
  Kennedy candidacy and, 118–25
  St. Benedict Center and, 71–81, 84
  Vietnam and, 140, 148–54
  see also specific groups
Roman Empire, 19–20
Roof, Wade Clark, 180
Roosevelt, Franklin D., 86
"Root Is Man, The" (Macdonald), 29
Roozen, David A., 170–71
Roper, Elmo, 27
Roper Poll, 27, 33
Rosenzweig, Franz, 49
Ross, Roy G., 105–6
Roszak, Theodore, 154, 155
Rotenstreich, Nathan, 147
Ruether, Rosemary, 180
Rummel, Archbishop, 132

St. Benedict Center, 71–81, 84
St. Louis Review, 120
Saturday Evening Post; 33

satyagraha, 116
Sayre, Francis B., Jr., 121
Schapiro, Meyer, 31
Schindler, Alexander M., 167–68
Schlesinger, Arthur, Jr., 91
Schulberg, Budd, 40, 178
Schuller, Robert, 179–80
science:
    atomic bomb and, 29–31
    religion vs., 15, 21, 31, 35
scientific naturalism, debate over,
    29–30, 43
Scopes "monkey trial," 21, 57
Second Assembly of the World
    Council of Churches, 62
Second Great Awakening, 20
Secular City, The (Cox), 134–35,
    171
secular humanism, 171–75, 178
Seduction of the Spirit, The (Cox),
    171
Self and Dramas of History, The
    (Niebuhr), 45–46
self-help, inner peace and, 33–35,
    138
Senate, U.S., 95–100
"Service to the Front" program
    (CBS radio), 32
Seven Storey Mountain, The
    (Merton), 37–38
Sheen, Fulton, 26, 37, 72, 92, 138
sit-ins, 108–12, 128
Six-Day War, 144–48, 158
Slaves of the Immaculate Heart of
    Mary, 80, 82–83, 84
Sloan, John E., 109
Smith, Al, 21, 118
Smith, Bailey, 160–62, 164–69,
    177
Snyder, Gary, 154, 155
Social Gospel, 21, 107, 115–17
Social Science Research Council,
    33
Society of Jesus, see Jesuits
Sollors, Werner, 177–78
Sorensen, Ted, 118, 121, 123, 124
Southern Baptist Convention, 60–
    61, 160, 162, 164–67
Southern Christian Leadership
    Conference (SCLC), 114
Soviet Union, 33, 35, 44, 64–65,
    91–92, 168, 169

Spellman, Francis Cardinal, 26, 38,
    118, 119, 138, 150, 151
Sperry, Willard L., 57–58
Spike, Robert W., 128
spiritual politics, use of term, 18
Stahlman, James G., 109
"Statement of Religious Liberty in
    Relation to the 1960 National
    Campaign," 124
Stepinac, Cardinal, 88
Stevenson, Adlai, 87
Stevenson, George S., 35
Straus, Roger, 44
Strauss, Gerald, 17
Stringfellow, William, 127–30,
    137, 140, 152–53
Student Volunteer Movement, 21
Study of History, A (Toynbee), 35–
    36
Suburban Captivity of the
    Churches (Winter), 117
Sunday, Billy, 55, 66, 101, 102
Supreme Court, U.S., 110, 172,
    174
Synagogue Council of America,
    125–26

Tanenbaum, Marc, 161, 165, 166
Tate, Allen, 31
Teachings of Don Juan, The
    (Castaneda), 155–56
textbooks, secular humanism and,
    172–73
theology:
    Death of God, 133–34, 135, 139
    Judeo-Christian tradition and,
    44–50
    of religious sects vs. state, 18–19
Third Force, in Christianity, 106–7
Third Great Awakening, 21
Thomism, 26–27, 30, 38, 51
Thomsen, Judge, 152
Thoreau, Henry David, 150, 151
Thurmond, Strom, 56
Tillich, Paul, 30, 31, 47, 50, 51,
    137, 138
Time magazine, 56, 133
Tobian, Milton, 160–61, 162, 167,
    168
toleration, religious, 15, 19–20, 77
totalitarianism, 42, 43–44, 91–92,
    95

totalitarianism (*cont.*)
  see also Communism; Soviet
  Union
Toynbee, Arnold, 35–36
Truman, Harry S., 23–24, 64,
  119
tschuvah, 50–51
Tugwell, Rexford, 28

*Uneasy Conscience of Modern
  Fundamentalism, The*
  (Henry), 59
Union Seminary Quarterly Review,
  61–62
Union Theological Seminary, 61,
  107
United Jewish Appeal, 144
United Presbyterian Church, 59, 60

Vagnozzi, Egidio, 118
Vahanian, Gabriel, 133
Van Buren, Paul, 133
Van Den Haag, Ernest, 95
Vanderbilt, Harold, 113
Vanderbilt University, 109–13,
  116
Van Dusen, Henry P., 25, 102, 106,
  145, 170
*Varieties of Religious Experience,
  The* (James), 176
Vatican II, 83, 84, 126, 133
Velde, Harold, 88
Vietnam war, 140, 146, 148–54
Vinci, Leonardo da, 25
Vital Center, The (Schlesinger), 91

Walsh, David, 80
Waugh, Evelyn, 79–80

We Hold These Truths (Murray),
  51–52
Weiss-Rosmarin, Trude, 43–44
Wesley, John, 65
West, Ben, 109
What Makes Sammy Run?
  (Schulberg), 40
*When Bad Things Happen to Good
  People* (Kushner), 179
Whitefield, George, 65
"Whither bound?" (Graham
  sermon), 67
*Why the Conservative Churches
  Are Growing* (Kelley), 170
Wilder, Amos, 42, 46
Wilderness Revolt, The (Pike and
  Kennedy), 141
Williams, J. Paul, 94–95, 98
Wills, Garry, 134
Wilson, Grady, 56
Winter, Gibson, 117
Witness (Hiss), 93–94
World Council of Churches (WCC),
  58, 59, 61, 62, 84, 120
World Evangelical Fellowship, 60
World War I, 22, 32
World War II, 22, 91
  antifascism and, 41–44
  atomic bomb in, 23–31, 36, 73–
  74
Wright, G. Ernest, 45
Wright, John, 76, 77–79

"Your Flesh Should Creep" (Alsop
  and Alsop), 32–33
Youth for Christ (YFC), 55, 171

Zhukov, Marshall, 44

ABOUT THE AUTHOR

Mark Silk is a reporter for the Atlanta *Journal-Constitution*. He has also taught at Harvard, edited the *Boston Review*, and written for *The New York Times Magazine*, *The New York Times Book Review*, and *The Boston Globe*. He has a Ph.D. in history from Harvard and is the coauthor, with Leonard Silk, of *The American Establishment*. He lives with his wife and son in Decatur, Ga.

DATE DUE

APR 30 1990		
APR 30 1998		
GAYLORD		PRINTED IN U.S.A.